TORRIDON
A WALKER'S GUIDE

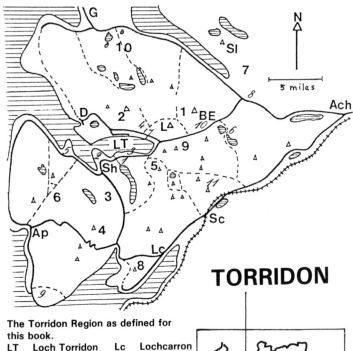

TORRIDON

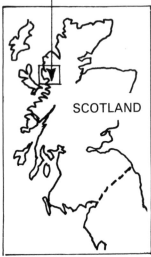

The Torridon Region as defined for this book.

LT	Loch Torridon	Lc	Lochcarron
Sh	Shieldaig	Ap	Applecross
Ach	Achnasheen	D	Diabeg
Sc	Strathcarron	G	Gairloch

Mountains

L	Liathach
BE	Beinn Eighe
SI	Slioch

The remainder should be found, from the map references given in the text, on the appropriate Ordnance Survey 1:50,000 sheets Nos. 19, 24 and 25.

Walks

The location of the recommended walks are shown by numbers: EASY WALKS 1-11 in *italic figures*; LONG WALKS 1-10 in **bold figures**.

TORRIDON

A WALKER'S GUIDE

**ELEVEN EASY WALKS
TEN LONG OR HIGH LEVEL WALKS
THIRTY-THREE SUMMITS
OVER TWO THOUSAND FEET**

by

PETER BARTON

2 POLICE SQUARE, MILNTHORPE, CUMBRIA LA7 7PY
www.cicerone.co.uk

© Peter Barton 1989
ISBN 1 85284 022 6
First published 1989
Reprinted 1991,1993,1995
Revised reprint 1999, 2004

PETER BARTON was born in London in 1921 and served in the army throughout the war. He attended a London Art School and subsequently studied medicine and dentistry and became an oral and maxillo-facial surgeon in Oxford. In 1983 he resigned his surgical appointment in order to live and paint full-time in the Torridon region and explore its mountains.

Front Cover: Liathach across Loch Bharanaichd
('loch varranch' - the loch of the long coarse grass')

Warning

Mountainous regions are rough and can be dangerous, particularly in bad weather and the author, the publisher and estate landlords cannot be held in any way responsible for any hazard or mishaps which may occur. Such warnings are necessary but accidents in this area have been few. So be careful and enjoy your walking.

It is necessary specifically to warn readers again that in bad weather and under winter conditions these mountains can be dangerous and expeditions onto them should only be undertaken by experienced hill walkers. If you have no experience it is better to learn hill walking technique on more populous mountains where you will not be alone, but in the Torridon region, in fine weather, to start on, I would suggest Beinn Damh and Tom na Gruagaich of Beinn Alligin. If you feel, after walking among these mountains, that I have exaggerated the difficulties, so much the better.

Advice to Readers

Readers are advised that whilst every effort is taken by the author to ensure the accuracy of this guidebook, changes can occur which may affect the contents. It is advisable to check locally on transport, accommodation, shops etc but even rights-of-way can be altered and, more especially overseas, paths can be eradicated by landslip, forest fires or changes of ownership.

CONTENTS

INTRODUCTION

I first started hill walking in the Lake District in my early fifties, and came to live in Shieldaig on Loch Torridon in 1983. These notes, describing the easiest and safest ways to reach the tops of the Torridon mountains, were originally intended for friends using our cottage. It seemed that they might be useful to other visitors with hill walking enthusiasm and experience, visiting Torridon for the first time; the sort of folk who are properly equipped and able to use map and compass, who may, for example, have enjoyed climbing Great Gable, Tryfan or The Cobbler by the easier routes, but prefer not to risk their lives or frighten themselves by exposure in precipitous places and narrow ridges.

Poucher's excellent guide *The Scottish Peaks* deals with only six of the thirty-one mountains over two thousand feet in the Torridon region which, for this purpose, I have interpreted widely to include the two hundred square miles south west of Loch Maree and north of the Achnasheen-Achnashellach-Lochcarron road, but including Slioch and its environs (See p.2).

I am upset by steep scree and exposed mountain routes that many others find merely 'interesting'. In the Wainwright tradition I have explored these mountains alone, looking for the easiest, and not necessarily the shortest, routes to their summits. Unlike most of the Cumbrian and Welsh peaks, the majority of these mountains do not have paths or walkers' tracks up them, but the many excellent stalkers' paths take one deep into wild country and often give a flying start to an ascent. But walkers in Torridon have to accustom themselves to free-ranging over heather, grass, rock and marsh. A lot of the lower ground is wet, but in my experience, perfectly safe to cross as long as one looks where on is putting one's feet, as mountain walkers should always do. Occasional black peat bogs, with miniature cliffs and sullen countenance, can look menacing, but they are easily circumvented and, in fact, are often quite hard. In wet places just tread on the grass and heather (but not on moss) and you will not sink more than a few inches. Generally when free-ranging, the going is much better over 1,000 feet and the higher the better, where there is little heather and the grass gets shorter and rock comes to predominate. However, heather is excellent non-slip stuff for descending steep muddy slopes.

One other warning is appropriate. A number of burns and rivers, which are easy to cross in dry weather, may become difficult or even dangerous in spate (after heavy rain or melting snows) when even working one's way hundreds of yards up or down stream may fail to resolve the problem. In these conditions be prepared to wade. Never wade in bare feet but carry spare socks in your haversack if you prefer walking with dry feet. Two heavy-duty polythene bags tied above the knees will help keep your feet dry, if you can be bothered to carry them. Rugged types simply wade and walk with wet feet for the rest of the day. Where streams ar steep and torrential, it may be better to call it a day: *N.B. Stream crossings can be dangerous.*

All the routes described make reference to the standard Ordnance Survey 1:50.000 maps: - sheets 19 (Gairloch and Ullapool), 24 (Raasay, Applecross and Loch Torridon) and 25 (Glen Carron), and the appropriate sheet should be carried on all these walks. The sketch maps in this book are only intended to facilitate reference to the proper Ordnance Survey sheets when reading the text. In the sketch maps stalker's and the other paths are shown as *broken lines*, the recommended free-ranging routes are shown as *dotted lines*. I have adopted the mountain and place names as printed on the O.S. 1:50,000 sheets, although there are some inconsistencies to be found in these. I have also offered approximate phonetic spellings and English translations for certain of the Gaelic names as they arise in the text (see Appendix. p.163).

Most of the expeditions assume that you have transport, and those which do not require it are indicated and are written as though Shieldaig is the starting point. The 'climbs' often involve descending again by the route of your ascent, which builds in a considerable safety factor if you are new to the area and also the comfort and pleasure of returning over familiar territory. This, I find, is never boring, as the spectacular views are just the opposite of what you have enjoyed going up. Please always tell someone where you are going and when you expect to be back (write it down on a card so there is no vagueness), stick to your stated plans and report your return. Should a search party ever have to look for you it is a courtesy to them that they should have some idea, where, within two hundred square miles, they should start looking. A rescue team in the Lake District spent forty-eight hours looking for two girls who turned up in Portsmouth.

I have researched these routes carefully so as not to mislead you, but features change over the years and I apologise for any unintentional errors that there may be. If you find anything that is wrong, I shall be pleased if you will let me know via the publisher, then I shall go and have another look for myself and make the necessarry corrections. Some of the high places in Torridon are vast complicated wildernesses so do not attempt ascents in bad weather or when there are bad forecasts. Should low cloud begin to threaten on your way up, a few well-chosen compass bearings, taken directly, and noted down on a scrap of paper can prove very helpful in the event of a subsequent mist-out, and also draw one's attention to the appearance of key landmarks *as they will appear on your way down*. Always write down the time at which you take these bearings in these circumstances. Maybe I am an old fuss-pot, but I always carry a heavy-duty survival bag, first aid, emergency ratios, torch, whistle, compasses, watch and maps and some spare warm clothing, winter and summer. Fortunately, water is plentiful in the Highlands and the sheep keep low.

We are permitted to walk these hills. In return for this privilege, it is a matter of courtesy to respect the deer-stalking season. The extent of this period is somewhat variable and also varies with estates, but September/October is the most important time (se p.165). Freedom to walk and climb the summits and southern aspects of Beinn Alligin, Beinn Dearg, Beinn Eighe and the whole of Liathach is granted at all times. Usually walking on the *paths* on other estates is accepted and often notices are displayed saying so. Stalking does not take place every day during the season and information can be obtained by enquiring at, or telephoning, the appropriate estate office. Although we may generally walk freely in the Highlands, providing we observe local restrictions and commit no nuisance or damage, the walks and ascents described in this book do not guarantee public right-of-way. Besides deer stalking, grouse shooting and fishing should be respected. Details are given, where relevant, in the text and in the Appendix.

Walking in the mountains of Torridon can be good in winter as the west coast climate is not harsh. Fresh snow is a delight to tread, but beware of cornices on the ridges. An ice-axe should be carried and crampons make snow walking easier. However it should be borne in mind that snow slopes, particularly at higher altitudes, may become glacial with a surface of hard ice, when even quite gentle slopes can be extremely dangerous if lying above crags. Such icy snowfields may persist on the northern aspects of the mountains into May and June. What may look like small patches from road level are often surprisingly extensive at 3,000 feet and may be difficult or dangerous obstacles when frozen hard. Summer and winter weather in the Highlands is always beautiful with blue skies predominating, to which assertion the numerous Highland calendars bear constant witness. The weather only turns foul when there are visitors.

DEER FENCES: These new high-wire and stake fences are being erected in the interests of reafforestation of certain areas by the native Scots Pine, Birch and Rowan. The fences are there to keep the **deer and sheep** out to prevent the trees from being eaten when only delicate young shoots - the fences are not there to keep walkers out, and high styles are usually placed at convenient places to allow walkers in. For example you will encounter such new high fences (but with convenient stiles) across the main saddle of Beinn Sheildaig (p.134); surrounding the new afforestation on the track to Loch na h-Oidche (p. 75); on the descent from An Fur (p.57); on the southern flanks of Liathach as seen from Glen Torridon (but not obstructing the usual ascent track up the mountain); but actually *blocking* the final ascent to the summit of the An Sgurr (p.71). However, the general plan is to dismantle these fences after about 12 years when they have done their job and the trees have become established, so the region will not be indefinitely disfigured by the fences, and a few areas of new forest will add to the general fineness of the region.

CAIRNS: These are, of course, removable stone structures, but I only refer to those marking summits or particular points of importance on certain routes, where they are likely to be left alone - if you fail to find one you are relying on to locate yourself, refer to your map.

CAR PARKING: The previous very great difficulty in finding somewhere to park your car in Incheril before setting out to climb Slioch as been solved by the provision of a generous but out-of-sight car park at the end of the track leading to the Heights of Kinlochewe (it is clearly signposted). But certain other squeeze-your-car-in spots have been rendered inadequate by road widening (see parking spot p3 on page 32 - but p4 is still available at the time of writing). Likewise my advice for parking on p.160 for Carn Breac has been made a nonsense because of the creation of a new road at this spot.

BRIDGES: From time to time these get swept away by winter storms, but are usually rebuilt by the Estate, but not always (as over Loch Coulin - p.29)

INTRODUCTION TO REPRINT 2004

After living alone for 18 years (from 1983) in a cottage in Shieldaig, now in my eighties, I developed the first signs of Parkinson's disease, and as this progressed somewhat I came to find it impossible to do any more hill walking. Indeed, Easy Walk 1 came to be quite beyond me. For this reason, I considered it best to return to Oxford from whence I had come, to live in a flat in sheltered housing and to be nearer members of my family. An additional impulse to move was that I found it difficult simply to sit and look at all those mountains, which when I first arrived in Shieldaig seemed a bit overwhelming to the hill walker I had lately become, but which, after much exploring and revisiting had become my friends.

This edition has, with the help of hill walking friends, been brought up to date as far as possible. This has to rely upon my belief that the actual "tops" don't alter much with the passage of time. But certain things at lower levels seem to be open to constant changes, and if, on any of my recommended walks or ascents you come across changes that I don't know about, please take this as part of the spirit of adventure in exploring these magnificent mountains, or inform the publisher of this guide if you consider it to be important.

Good walking and ascending Peter Barton

EASY WALKS

		Total Distance in Miles	Total Time in Hours	Page
EW1	Falls of Balgy and Loch Damh (Shieldaig)	2¼	1	12
EW2	The Shieldaig Peninsula (Shieldaig)	2½	1½	16
EW3	West Lodge. S.Shore Upper Loch Torridon (Shieldaig)	min 2	1	19
		max 5	2½	
EW4	Coire Mhic Nobuil (Alligin)	3	1½	23
EW5	Ardheslaig to Kenmore, old bridle path (Applecross Peninsula)	4	2½	25
EW6	Coulin Estate, Loch Clair and Loch Coulin (Glen Torridon)	5	2½	28
EW7	Torridon (Fasag) to Inveralligin (N.Shore Upper Loch Torridon).	min 3	1½	30
		max 8	4	
EW8	Heights of Kinlochewe (Incheril)	max 10	5	35
EW9	Toscaig to Airigh-drishaig (S.Applecross)	min 2½	1½	38
		max 8	5	
EW10	The Coire an Laoigh of Beinn Eighe (Glen Torridon)	3	3-4	42
EW11	The cold hollow of Fuar Tholl (from Achnashellach)	6	5	44

EASY WALKS

The walks are presented in ascending order of length and difficulty, taking these two factors in combination, and mostly make use of good paths, tracks and quiet roads. For *Walks 1-7* stout walking shoes should prove adequate in dry weather, but after rain many paths become marshy and boots are always to be preferred. *Walks 8-11* take the walker into wilder and higher country and the precincts of big mountains and should not be undertaken by inexperienced walkers in bad weather. For these walks rainwear, spare warm clothing, food and water, maps and compass should be carried and boots should be worn.

As well as references to various sketch maps provided in the text, appropriate Ordnance Survey map references are also given. The relevant Ordnance Survey maps (1:50,000) are:

> Sheet 19   Gairloch
> Sheet 24   Raasay, Applecross and Loch Torridon
> Sheet 25   Glen Carron

Distances are given in miles and kilometres and times assume progress at a steady pace with occasional stops.

It is essential constantly to watch one's step when walking over rough paths and rough ground, always stopping when admiring the scenery. Such vigilance minimises the risk of stumbling or slipping. Wet rocks and the exposed roots of trees are particular hazards and, of course, ice and ice on rocks (verglas) in winter. The author has taken care in selecting and describing these walks but some features will inevitably change with the passage of time and each individual must take responsibility for his or her own safety.

EW1: Falls of Balgy and Loch Damh

Nearest village: Shieldaig
2¼ miles.   3.6km.   1 hour.   Can be extended.
O.S. sheet 24.   (Map p.14)

The short River Balgy serves as the outlet for Loch Damh into Loch Torridon, Loch Damh itself draining the territory at the southern end of the loch (Ceann loch damh or head of loch damh). From the loch

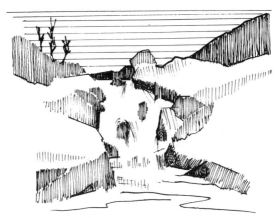

the fresh water tumbles delightfully down a rocky gorge in a series of falls where the salmon and sea trout, coming from the sea water of Loch Torridon, may be seen leaping during the months of June, July and August. A triangular walk, up by the falls over a somewhat marshy and rough path and a return via a good track and then the road makes a pleasant but short expedition, ideal on a summer evening. It can, however, be extended several miles up the excellent track running along the E side of Loch Damh if desired. Stout shoes are adequate in dry weather but in wet weather the Balgy river path becomes marshy in places.

Leave your car on either side of the Balgy bridge on the N side of the road (A). The bridge is situated 2½ miles from Shieldaig on the Shieldaig-Torridon road at 847544. The path commences about 75 yards east of the bridge (on the Torridon side) through the clearly marked gate. After crossing flat somewhat marshy ground for 300 yards you reach the lowest part of the falls at a good vantage point to see the salmon leaping in season. The fishing rights on this river are strictly reserved. Please also respect the quiet of the riverside when anglers are present during the fishing season.

The path ascends and there follows a short stretch where, although wide, it runs near the edge of the gorge and it is advisable to have young children under control in this section. After descending, the path runs close to the river's edge to reach a little beach and a new boat-house (B). A wire fence juts out into the loch but is easily negotiated, using the conveniently placed boulders above water level. You now have a commanding view of Loch Damh dominated by the Sgurr

13

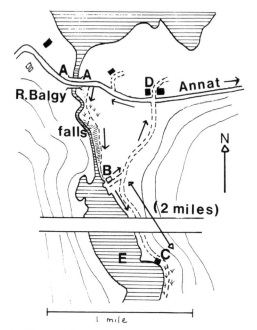

**Walk from the River Balgy bridge (A) up the Balgy falls to Loch Damh (E).
Salmon leap here in the summer.**

na Bana Mhoraire of Beinn Damh to your left, and the NE flank of
Beinn Shieldaig to your right. At the end of the loch and in the
distance stands Sgurr a' Gharaidh.

Passing in front of the boat-house you will come to a new track
which leads up from the boat-house to the main track which runs
along the loch side. This provides excellent walking as far as the lodge
house at Doire Damh 2 miles up the loch (C), if you wish to extend
your walk. Beyond that point the track changes to a small path which
mostly keeps to the water's edge and is inclined to be marshy and
overgrown in places.

Having reached the main track, and if you do not want to walk along
the loch side, turn L, walking ¾ mile back to the road. At first the
track crosses moorland and finally runs between rhododendrons to
reach the road opposite West Lodge (D). During this part of the walk
the view is dominated by the summits of Beinn Alligin and Beinn

14

Dearg on the other side of Loch Torridon. Once you reach the road it is a pleasant downhill stroll for ¾ mile back to Balgy bridge where you left your car.

WALKING ROUND LOCH DAMH

A walk right round Loch Damh is a more considerable undertaking. The path between the lodge at Doire Damh and Ceann loch damh is a further 2½ miles and is small, uneven and wet in places. At Ceann loch damh the red river (Abhainn Dearg) has to be crossed. There is no bridge. In dry weather it is easy to cross the wide but very shallow bed by jumping from boulder to boulder but in spate wading is necessary. Once across, a good track (1 mile) leads from the house to the Kishorn-Shieldaig road. From here it is a 4¾ mile walk back along the road in Glen Shieldaig to Shieldaig village, unless you hitch a lift or have arranged transport. A much more adventurous route is to ascend the easy slopes at the S end of Beinn Shieldaig NW of Ceann loch damh (staring at 855477) and return along the broad summit ridge of Beinn Sheildaig, see p.133, traversing the first two summits at 849503 (439m) and 843514 to reach the saddle at 838518; and thence down rough ground to regain the NW shore and 'jetties' of Loch Damh (848532) returning to the road via the marshy path on the W side of the Balgy falls. See also the ascent of Beinn Shieldaig (S7) p.131. This is a major undertaking (8 hours) only suitable for fully equipped and experienced mountain walkers.

Easiest of all is to take the postal service minibus (Duncan Maclellan) from Shieldaig bus shelter, adjacent to the Tigh an Eilean Hotel at 10.15am*. (not Sundays). Ask to be put down at the top of Glen Shieldaig opposite the drive to Kinloch Damh. Walk down the drive to the white house, cross the river and thence take up and follow the path along the E side of Loch Damh to the Balgy falls. From the Balgy bridge it is a 2½ mile road walk back to Sheildaig, a corner of which can be cut by using the old track which commences above the large grey rock to the left of the stone building 100 yards west of the bridge.

I give this information because many visitors ask if it is possible to walk round Loch Damh. It is a serious undertaking and spare pairs of socks will increase comfort if the river at Ceann loch damh has to be waded.

Beinn Damh - 'Ben darv' - the stag mountain.
Sgurr na Bana Mhoraire - 'Sgoorr na bana-voraire' - peak of the lord's lady.
Sgurr a' Gharaidh - 'Sgoorr a yarray' - peak of the beast's lair.

* Check up-to-date time.

Loch Damh from near the head of the Balgy river.

EW2: The Shieldaig Peninsula

Nearest village: Shieldaig
2½ miles. 4km. 1½-2 hours.
O.S. sheet 24. (Map p.17)

The Shieldaig peninsula juts out into Loch Torridon dividing it into Upper and Lower lochs at the narrows. There is a good track for the first mile but this becomes a path which later divides. Parts of both the subsequent paths are muddy in places after wet weather. You can walk to the end of either path and the views are very fine. It is also fairly easy to cross over higher ground, which is rough and usually wet, in order to complete a full circuit of the end of the peninsula.

The walk starts in Shieldaig (A). The track goes up beside Shieldaig school (B), but before commencing the walk it is worthwhile going a hundred yards down the private road beyond the school to see the old stone preaching wall. The views of Shieldaig village across the bay from this road are very pretty.

Follow the track past the school for a mile and past two bays on your left, with fine views out to sea. Harris (Outer Hebrides) is visible on a clear fine day. Throughout the walk, particularly related to the bays, you will see the stone ruins of old crofters' and coopers' cottages. After a mile the path divides (C). I suggest you take the right fork, whether you intend just to go to the end of the peninsula or to make

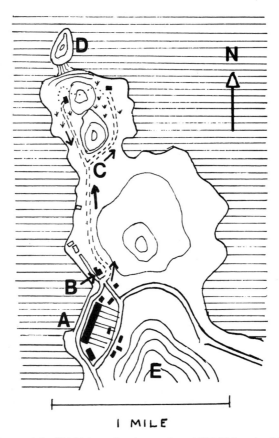

I MILE

**Walk round the Shieldaig peninsula, starting at Shieldaig school (B).
There are fine views out to sea and up Loch Torridon.**

the round trip, since you will already have enjoyed fine views out to
sea and the R path now offers the best views of Loch Torridon and its
mountains.

At the end of the path is a grassy meadow leading down to a
cottage. If you wish to make the circular walk, find your way over the
promontory, starting at the wooded section (lower left) in marshy
ground. Please respect the privacy of the owners of this and the other
cottage in case they are in residence. (The whole peninsula in fact

belongs to the owner of the cottage situated on the W side.)

It is not possible to go round the end of the peninsula at sea level, but once up on the promontory you will pick up a marshy path leading you across. At the other end the path divides. The left branch brings you down very close to the house. Take the R branch which seems to lead up to a cliff edge, but, in fact, leads to an easy grass and heather ledge by which you can safely descend.

You can cross to the island (D) at low tide, if you wish. It gives good views of the narrows between Upper and Lower Loch Torridon. Directly across the water is the rocky Diabaig peninsula.

Pick up the rather marshy path beyond the second cottage, which quickly improves, and will lead you back to the place where the track divides (C) and thence back to Shieldaig school. On the return journey the view is dominated by the precipitous N buttresses of Beinn Shieldaig (E) ahead.

In summer this walk is made fragrant by the scent of wild myrtle bushes. The resident wild animals, who will watch your progress throughout, are sheep (not dangerous).

Shieldaig derives from the Norse Sild-vig, meaning herring bay.

Upper Loch Torridon and Liathach from the Shieldaig peninsula walk.

EW3: West Lodge, Loch Torridon, Loch Torridon Hotel

Nearest village: Shieldaig and Annat
2-5 miles. 3.2-8km. 1-2½ hours.
O.S. sheet 24. (Map p.19)

This is a delightful walk, in fine weather, among rhododendrons, woodlands and open spaces, along the south shore of upper Loch Torridon and can be made short or longer as desired.

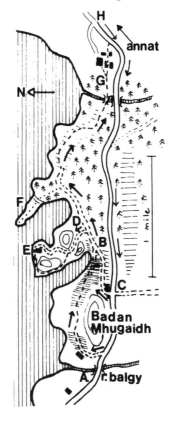

Walk along the S shore of Loch Torridon from West Lodge (C) or Badan Mhugaidh (A).

For the commencement of the longer and more adventurous walk leave your car by the N side of the road at the Balgy bridge walk 30 yards up the road at 846544 (A). From the bridge walk 30 yards up the road towards Annat and Torridon and take the track on the LHS of the road which leads to a house and stable. Ignore the track from West Lodge which dissects your route and continue generally east above Loch Torridon when you will have fine views of the N Torridon mountains. As you reach the first bay (Ob Gorm Beag) you will be joined by the far wider track coming down from West Lodge to your right (B) and the walking will become easier again. During this first section you will see the ruins of several old croft houses and barns.

Alternatively, for a shorter walk, leave your car near West Lodge (C) (857542). Go through the iron gates (which may be closed, but not locked), and walk down the track among rhododendrons. After ¼ mile you will be joined by the earlier track from Badan Mhugaidh mentioned above.

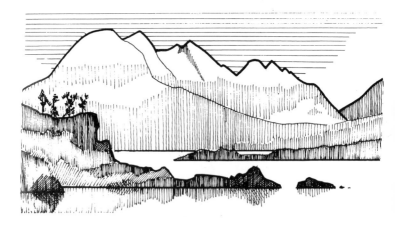

Beinn Alligin seen across Loch Torridon from the West Lodge path.

As you approach the first bay you will see the rows of buoys stretched across the water marking the site of the mussel farm. As you enter more open scrub land you will reach a gate on the L (D), across a track which leads out to the first peninsula and the old croft cottage and fishing sheds at its tip. The shortest walk is to stroll out to the end of the track and shoreline and then back, by the way you came, to the road; but if you plan to do the full walk it is still well worth making this 40 minute detour. This branch track first passes through a miniature, but impressive, rocky gorge and then winds to the right and down to the cottage at the shore (E). Follow the track beyond the cottage to the shore and past the fishing sheds where you can continue along a small path which leads W and then S round the promontory to rejoin the main track before it enters the gorge.

To complete the shortest walk retrace your steps back to the road. Otherwise continue W along the original track, with fine views of Beinn Alligin, Beinn Dearg and the Sgurr a' Chadail, the most westerly peak of Liathach, across the loch.

As you approach the second bay (Ob Gorm Mor) you will pass through an old estate wall and gateway, dramatically attached to a large vertical boulder close to the loch side, and you will see the second, flatter peninsula stretching far out into the loch (F). You can decide whether you wish to make this second detour, where you will have to find your own way over the initial rocky and wooded area (there is a vestigial path leading off through the rhododendron clumps to the left). It is worth the trouble as the tip of this peninsula stands well out into Loch Torridon, offering fine views and the chance of seeing seals, herons and other shore and sea birds.

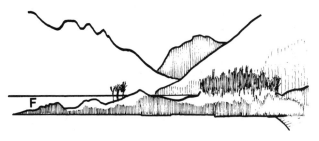

Ob Gorm Mor peninsula

After exploring this second peninsula, or if you elected not to do so, proceed E down the tracks for a further half mile after which, for the next mile, the going is less pleasant as a path, which may be muddy, is somewhat overgrown by rhododendrons. Further extensive clearance of the rhododendrons between this point and the Loch Torridon Hotel is in progress, but I cannot say when this work will be completed (Nov. 2003). However, it is worth persisting in order to enjoy the spectacular views on your walk back to West Lodge along the road.

In due course the path becomes wider and the rhododendrons thinner, and suddenly you will come again into the open with Beinn na h-Eaglaise ahead. Try to ignore the derelict car to your left and the view will widen to reveal part of the mountain range of south Torridon (from left to right, Seanna Mheallan, Sgurr na Lochaine Uaine and Beinn Liath Mhor).

Crossing a wooden bridge over the river (Allt Drochaid Coire Roill) the track divides (G). Take the right fork to the stables; the left leads to Loch Torridon Hotel. Immediately after the stables you come to the Beinn Damh bar (L), (open all year), and the hotel gift shop, which also functions part-time as a post office (but may be intermittently closed), and a petrol station (seasonal).

When you reach the road (H) turn right and climb the bend to cross the bridge over the river you crossed shortly before. This bridge and road to Shieldaig were opened in 1963. Previously there was only a track joining Torridon to Shieldaig. You now have a 2-2½ mile road walk, according to where you left your car. The views from the road are magnificent, but since, particularly in summer, there will be some traffic, walk on the right-hand side to face oncoming vehicles. As the road rises gently the views of Liathach, with the village of Fasag nestling beneath the Mullach am Rathain, and of Beinn Dearg and Beinn Alligin, unfold. After the highest point you will see the village of Inveralligin farther up the loch on the far side and, on a clear day, the table mountains (the Quirang) of northern Skye beyond the vista of loch and promontories which stretch before you.

Badan Mhugaidh - 'bad-an-vugie' - Mungo's clump or the gloomy clump.
Ob Gorm Beag - 'ob-gorm-bek' - little blue bay.
Ob Gorm Mor - big blue bay.

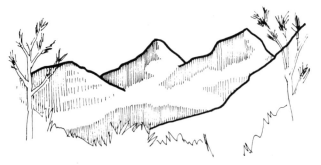

As you emerge from the rhododendrons near the Loch Torridon Hotel, Seanna Mheallan (left), Sgurr nan Lochan Uaine, Beinn Liath Mhor and the slopes of Beinn na h-Eaglaise (right) appear on the horizon.

EW4: A stroll up Coire Mhic Nobuil beneath Beinn Alligin. (From the Beinn Alligin car park)

3 miles. 4.2km. 1½ hours (to the deer post and back).
O.S. sheet 24. (Map p.24)

This walk, on the N side of Upper Loch Torridon, takes you by a good but rough path into wild country under the towering ramparts of Beinn Alligin, Beinn Dearg and Sgorr a' Chadail the most westerly peak of Liathach. It can be extended as far as you like.

Beinn Dearg and the solitary post at the head of the Coire Mhic Nobuil.

23

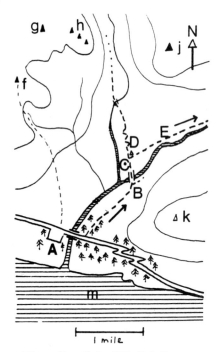

The walk up Coire Mhic Nobuil.
(f) - Tom na Gruagaich (g) - Sgurr Mhor (h) - Alligin Horns
(j) - Beinn Dearg (k) - Sgorr a' Chadaill, Liathach's most westerly peak
(m) - Loch Torridon.

Leave your car at the Beinn Alligin car park (A) 2½ miles west of Torridon village (Fasag) 869576. Walk back across the bridge over the deep gorge of the river (the Abhainn Coire Mhic Nobuil) and go up the path entering the wood immediately after the bridge on your left. The path ascends easily, at first in woodland and then in open country beside this beautiful tumbling river. Tom na Graugaich, the first peak of Beinn Alligin, rises majestically above you, followed by Sgurr Mhor and the serrated Alligin Horns. Ahead you will see the unwelcoming steep slopes of Beinn Dearg. After 1¼ miles the path crosses the river by a stout wooden bridge (B) and a hundred yards further along you will see an isolated wooden post standing in the heather 10 yards to the left of the path (C). The post is obviously being rubbed and, although overgrown in summer, a circle of muddy ground, marked by deer hoof prints appear each winter, so my guess is that deer find this a suitable post to scratch themselves on. The time will come of course, when this post will have rotted and disappeared.

A few yards farther on a cairn marks a division in the path. The path ahead (D), rougher and steeper, leads up the valley, between the Horns and Beinn Dearg's western flank (and beyond) and is the path used by hill walkers ascending or descending the Alligin Horns. The path to the right continues right round the northern aspect of Liathach to rejoin the road 6½ miles farther on. You will find this walk (8 miles in all) recommended in certain books, and the Ordnance Survey (1:25,000) map, *The Cuillin and Torridon Hills* shows a green dotted path which invites this expedition. In fact the path is good except for a miserable 1½ miles at its middle (between Lochan a' Chaorainn and Loch Grobaig) where it is very marshy and one has to negotiate black peat cliffs; no dangers but no enjoyment.

However, if you wish to extend your present walk the path continuing behind Liathach is good for another 1½ miles (E). The good parts of this whole path are, perhaps, better used as part of the walk round Beinn Alligin or to visit the Coire Mhic Fhearchair (see LONG WALKS 1 and 2, p.49 and p.52.

On your return you will enjoy fine views across Loch Torridon and of Loch Damh in the distance.

Coire Mhic Nobuil - 'corrie-vik-nobul' - corrie of the son of Nobuil.

EW5: Old Bridle Path, Ardheslaig to Kenmore. (Commences and ends at Ardheslaig on the Shieldaig to Applecross coast road)

4 miles.   6.4km.   2½ hours.
O.S. sheet 24. (Map p.27)

This delightful walk, which uses both tarmac road and good bridle path, takes one easily and safely on foot into wild country, offering a constantly changing environment and very impressive views of the Torridon mountains. Take your car along the Shieldaig to Applecross coast road (not over the Bealach na Ba) to Ardheslaig, which is about 5 miles from Shieldaig, at 783559. There are one or two suitable places to park your car on the left-hand side of the road 100 yards *before* you reach the Ardheslaig sign and turning (A). If you take your car beyond this point you will have to turn round and come back to avoid having to park it in an inconvenient place.

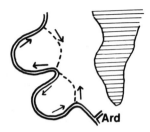

The walk can be varied in several ways but I think the most enjoyment may be had by making a figure of eight out of it. Walk north-west along the road beside the south-west shore of Loch Beag. As you round the corner you will see the old bridle path, in use until the new road was built in 1974, climbing up to your right. Join the bridle path just over the bridge to the driveway to the white house (B) and ascend. Where the new road reaches its highest point the old track has been virtually demolished for a quarter of a mile, so on your outward journey I suggest you leave the path and rejoin the road at the place where it is easiest to do this, 10 yards beyond an old milestone on your left (C). The possibility of not using the road at all at this point will be described for the return journey.

Proceed uphill for four hundred yards and then enjoy the 1½ miles of quiet road walking downhill past Loch na Creige (the loch of the crag). In summer there will be folk drifting past in cars, but for most of the way there is pleasant walking to be had on the grass and rock verge on the side of the road. In this section the road traverses a wild moorland bowl. There is a good chance of seeing deer.

After some bends the road descends and you will see the signpost on the right-hand side of the road indicating the emergence of the old bridle path onto the new road (D). The white cottages of Kenmore village are visible a few yards beyond this point and you may decide to walk the extra 1½ miles (there and back) before returning by the bridle track to Ardheslaig. This will add ¾ hour or so onto your walk.

Turning back down the old bridle path (D) you will cross a wooden bridge over a delightful burn and ascend up the side of a small valley of great charm with the burn running along the valley bottom on your right. (The first 100 yards of path beyond the bridge is somewhat overgrown by heather and bracken.) After ¾ mile the path bends and various small rocky and grassy eminences on either side invite an easy walk/scramble to one of their tops from which glorious views of upper

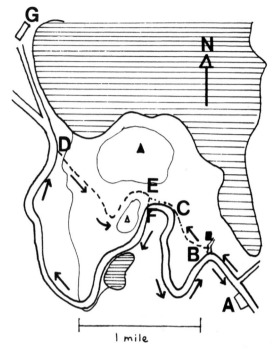

'Figure of 8 walk' from Ardheslaig (A) towards Kenmore (G)

Loch Torridon and the mountains may be obtained, but if you prefer not to leave the path it will, in due course, afford you similar views as you reach its summit (E).

The old bridle path now descends and a sharp right turn leads back to the road at (F), from whence a pleasant ½ mile saunter downhill, with spectacular views, will bring you back to Ardheslaig.

For more adventurous souls it is possible to rejoin the old bridle path by which you ascended by keeping below the road and using a somewhat eroded rough little path which still runs below the new road. This traverses steep ground and requires occasional scrambling over rocks to negotiate, but it is fun to do. Having crossed this section to reach C there is the alternative of returning to Ardheslaig keeping to the bridle path (and thus not completing the last limb of the figure of eight) or rejoining the road in order to do so

27

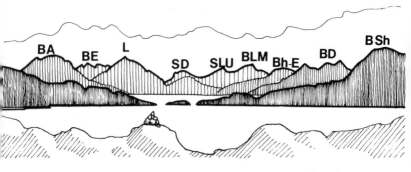

The panoramic view of the Torridon mountains and Loch Torridon as seen on easy walk 5. From the left to right:- Beinn Alligin, Beinn Eighe, Liathach, Sgurr Dubh, Sgurr nan Lochan Uaine, Beinn Liath Mhor, Beinn na h-Eaglaise, Beinn Damh and Beinn Shieldaig.

EW6: Coulin Estate. Loch Clair and Loch Coulin. (From upper Glen Torridon)

5 miles. 8km. 2½ hours.
O.S. sheet 25. (Map p.29)

The principal features of this walk are the beautiful lochs, in a setting of Scots pines, with fine views of Beinn Eighe. The entrance to the Coulin Estate is on the Kinlochewe to Torridon road, 3 miles SW of Kinlochewe (003582). There is room for 4-5 cars, if neatly parked, opposite the estate road (A). Watch out for the odd boulder and the concrete litter bin when reversing in.

Walk down the road toward Loch Clair, where a notice announces the Coulin Estate and 'no cars'. Cross the wooden bridge over the Allt Ghairbhe (B). Notice the fine view of Liathach to your R, so popular on Highland calendars. At the end of Loch Clair the wooden bridge on your R leads to the private part of the estate and a FOOTPATH sign directs you straight on past the intermediate lochan towards Loch Coulin. Close to the shore you will find a freshwater salmon farm which raises the fish, in fresh water, to the smolt stage.

Shortly after the commencement of Loch Coulin the road you are on curves upwards and to the left into the plantation and a second FOOTPATH sign directs you straight forward along the small foot-

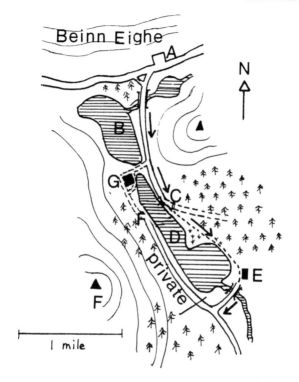

The lovely walk around the Coulin Estate takes you past lochs in a setting of Scots pines, and affords magnificent views of the Beinn Eighe range.

path you should take (C). Above you to your right Meall an Leathaid Mhoir (the hill of the big slope) (F) dominates.

For the next mile, if it has been wet, there will be places where those wearing shoes may wish they had boots, as you cross somewhat marshy ground. Find your way to reach the white lodge house ahead (E). After that, cross the wide wooden bridge over the River Coulin and you are back on a good track and road.

Walking up the W side of Loch Coulin, although now entering private land, it used to be the accepted practice for walkers to proceed up the west side of the loch as far as F where one could cross by an attractive footbridge back to C, thus completing a circular walk of Loch Coulin;

29

but the Estate demolished this bridge after it was damaged by winter storms. So you now have the option either to *trespass* right up to the Estate House and out-buildings, in order to complete the round trip, or to return up the east side of the loch, the way you came down. (The track proceeding southwards at the far end of Loch Coulin ultimately leads to a path going, via Coire Laire, all the (long) way to Achnashellach.)

This is a particularly lovely walk in midwinter on a fine day, when the range of Beinn Eighe's peaks are covered in glistening white snow.

Allt Ghairbhe - 'alt garve' - rough stream.

Beinn Eighe from Loch Clair.

EW7: Fasag to Inveralligin (North shores of Upper Loch Torridon)

Maximum 8 miles.   12.8km.   4 hours.
Minimum 3 miles.   4.8km.   1½ hours.
O.S. sheet 24.   (Map p.31)

I award this walk, so level and easy under the feet, the Golden Rose for its beauty, variability and grandeur. Proceeding along excellent bridle paths and single track roads, it offers beautiful lochside walking, fine woodland scenery, a church to visit, a coastal path, an intimate little village, and grand scenery with panoramic views of Loch Torridon and its mountains. What is more you can make it as long or as short as you like and it is still worth doing. On a fine day nothing could be better; but in the pouring rain .... well that is a different matter.

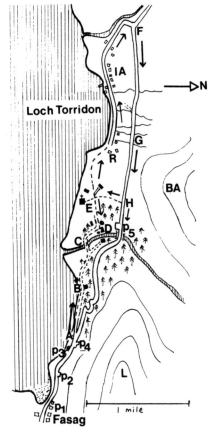

The walk from Fasag (Torridon) (F) to Inveralligin (IA) via Torridon House estate.

The full walk starts at Fasag village (more usually called Torridon these days), follows the road, bridle path, footpath and road, along the north shore of Upper Loch Torridon, to Inveralligin village and returns along the mountain road above Inveralligin to Fasag (total 8 miles, 4 hours) but a shorter version, as far as Torridon church and back, from car parking places 1 mile W of Fasag (3 miles, 1½ hours) is also worth doing.

1998: Parking at p3 is no longer practicable.

Park at Fasag p1, or at p2, or p4. There is nowhere to park beyond this point. (Please do not block the fish farm track to the shore nor the entrance to Torridon House.)

Turn down the private drive to Torridon House marked PUBLIC FOOTPATH TO INVERALLIGIN (A). You start by walking under wooded rocky cliffs and along the delightful shoreline. Throughout this walk keep a lookout for seals, porpoises, otters and various sea birds (ducks, divers, herons etc.). You pass a lodge house (B) and later a boat-house.

Bear left at the road fork (the right fork leads to Torridon House) and cross the iron and wood bridge (C) over the river (Allt Coire Mhic Nobuil) tumbling down to the loch from the mountains above. (The wooden planks on this bridge are sometimes very slippery in wet muddy weather, so be careful here.)

The bridle path now winds round to the right, past a cottage and house, to the stables/garages of the estate. Keep to the main track heading straight towards the green garage doors.

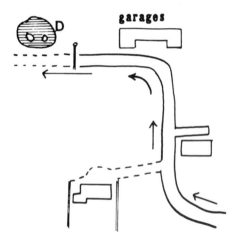

Bear left in front of the garages and pass through the gate and walk on by a lovely small lochan on your right surrounded by rhododendrons and containing two rhododendron islands (D).

Now you come into the open and follow a footpath to Torridon church (Church of Scotland) and old manse. Visit the church, noticing the little path which ascends to the road immediately opposite the path

1998: A new signposted path to Inveralligin, just over the bridge, avoids the estate buildings altogether.

to the church (E). The church, gaunt outside, but having a delightfully simple interior of plain timber and stone, is usually left open for visitors; just turn the big key in the lock, and lock again when you leave.

Now continue along the path, passing an old barn on your right. At this stage Beinn Alligin and Beinn Dearg, above the barn, begin to dominate the view.

But if you feel you have done enough you can instead return to your car, either back along the drive which you have already come along, or by going up the rough path to the road above. This path, inclined to be wet, is not very steep and commences exactly opposite the path down to the church, 45 paces east from the side track leading to the barn. When you reach the road turn right and walk back down the road, amid dramatic scenery, to your car. This short round trip takes, in all, about 1 hour 30 minutes.

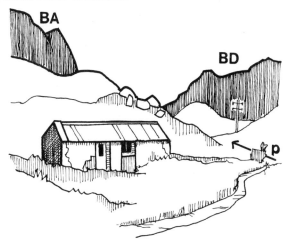

The old barn above Torridon church on the track to Inveralligin.
A path (p) leads up, 45 paces to the right from the track leading to the barn, to the road. Behind are Beinn Alligin (BA) and Beinn Dearg (BD).

If you have decided to continue you next come to a charming small headland and Rechullin, where you may be greeted by a few barking but friendly farm dogs. Walk past the farm, joining the coast road to Inveralligin. This stretch of the road is short but lovely; a rocky hillside with descending burns on your right and the loch on your left.

A degree of suburbanisation has occurred at Inveralligin which will not be to everyone's taste but the cluster of old cottages opposite the little pier is delightful.

The road curves to the right out of the village, and climbs beside a miniature gorge to reach the main Torridon-Diabaig road (F). Turn right. The next 2 miles of road walking offers a marvellous panoramic view of the Torridon mountains. You can never properly appreciate the beauties of this moorland road from inside a car, with Beinn Alligin towering above you on your left and the villages and loch away below you.

After a mile and a quarter you will come to a superbly placed roadside bench (G), which is a fine spot for a picnic lunch (Notice the old track down to the village, just before the bridge over a little burn, shortly before this).

You will appreciate how the ring of mountains are coming into view all round you. In fact, on this walk, at various times, you can see summits of all the surrounding Torridon mountains over 2,400 feet except for one, and there is a magic moment as you walk back towards Fasag, high on this road, when you can see all these mountains at one moment, though not all their summits.

These are, from your left (N) round to your right (S):

Beinn Alligin (Tom na Gruagaich)
Beinn Eighe (Ruadh Stac Mór and Sail Mhor)
Liathach (Sgurr a' Chadail and Mullach am Rathain)

At the head of the loch:

Sgurr nan Lochan Uaine
Beinn Liath Mhor
Sgorr Ruadh

Across the loch:

Beinn na h-Eaglaise (with Maol Chean Dearg behind)
An Ruadh Stac
Beinn Damh

and, of course:

Beinn Shieldaig (only 1,700ft.)

Only Sgurr Dubh is hidden.

A mile and three quarters after joining the Diabaig road turning (F), you will see a gate on the right-hand side and sign to THE CHURCH OF SCOTLAND (H). It is very pleasant to take this path, a little rough, not very steep but inclined to be wet, back down to the church and thence back through the estate the way you came, to your car, but the alternative, of staying on the road, is also very fine as it descends amid wooded and mountainous scenery.

I have walked widely in the Torridon region and have been to the summits of all its mountains, but I still rate this walk the most beautiful of all, when it is not raining.

Fasag - a dwelling or sheltered place.
Torridon - a way through or passage.

The eastern peaks of Glen Torridon. Left to right:- Sgurr nan Lochan Uaine, Beinn Liath Mhor and Sgorr Ruadh.

EW8: Heights of Kinlochewe. (Commences at Incheril by Kinlochewe)

10 miles. 16km. 5 hours. Ascent 1,000 feet.
O.S. sheet 19. (Map p.36) Keep strictly to the main path during the estate shooting season, mid-August to February.

Beyond and to the N of Loch Maree lies the wild mountainous region of the Fisherfield 'forest' (no trees) and this walk gives a glimpse of it across the splendid Lochan Fada (F). Consult you O.S. sheet 19 and you will find the area under consideration lying immediately to the N of Kinlochewe (026619).

The route follows an excellent track and finally path which leads one safely onto the edge of some of the region's wildest scenery. Take a map so that you can identify its famous mountains. You will return by the same track and therefore can make the walk as short or as long as you like. When you get as far as Loch Gleann na Muice (E) you will find out why Slioch (= spear) is so called. (Alternatively 'Sliabhach', place of slopes. The derivation is disputed.) The Kinlochewe Estate is efficiently run and shooting takes place on the open moorland, so please obey the request on the notice at the entrance to the estate to

Slioch from above the Heights of Kinlochewe.

stay on the paths.

Incheril (I) is a small hamlet ½ mile E of Kinlochewe. Park your car in the (signposted) car park in Incheril, which is situated conveniently near the track leading either to the Heights of Kinlochewe (to the right) or Slioch (to the left).

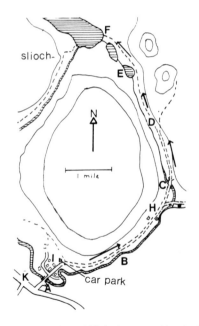

Walk from Incheril to the Heights of Kinlochewe and beyond for excellent views of the wild country round Lochan Fada.

Walk straight up the road (north-east) to the estate gate. For the next two miles you proceed on the level, with the river (Abhainn Bruachaig) on your right. About a mile up the road, where there is a curve in the river and it comes close to the road, cross the grass to the river bank to see the strange shapes and tunnels which the river waters have carved into the soft pinkish sandstone (B).

After 2 miles you will reach the Heights of Kinlochewe (H) passing some empty cottages (one delightfully placed on the river bank). You will see the well kept farmhouse to the right, but *take the ascending left fork* in the track.

The track now becomes rougher, crosses a wooden bridge over the river (C), and leads you, in 1¾ miles, to the top of the upper valley (Gleann na Muice) (D). Follow the path for a further 1½ miles until you reach Loch Gleann na Muice (E), Loch an Sgeireach and then the shores of Lochan Fada (F). Slioch is the first mountain to the L (west).

Return to Incheril by the same track.

Lochan Fada - 'Lohhan-farda' - long lochan.
Gleann na Muice - 'glen-na-muihh' - glen of the pig.
Lochan Sgeirach - 'lohhan-sgerrihh' - reef lochan.
Beinn Tharsuinn Chaol - 'Ben-tarsen-kyle' - transverse mountain of the narrows.
A' Mhaighdean - 'A' vuhh-vayn' - the maiden.
Mullach Coire Mhic Fhearchair - 'Mullahh-corrie-vik-errihher' - summit of the corrie of the son of Farquhar.

The panorama of mountains round Lochan Fada, from west to east:
a Slioch (Sgurr an Tuill Bhain). The 'spear' or place of slopes.
b Meall Daimh   c Sgurr Dubh (Beinn Lair beyond)   d Beinn Tharsuinn Chaol
e A' Mhaighdean (The Maiden)   f Beinn Tarsuinn
g Mullach Coire Mhic Fhearchair.

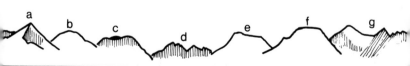

EW9: Toscaig to Airigh-drishaig (Ardrishaig). Commences at Upper Toscaig at the southern tip of the Applecross Peninsula

8 miles.   12.8km.   5 hours.   860 ft.

or **Toscaig to the River Toscaig gorge.**

2½ miles.   4km.   1½ hours.
O.S. sheet 24.   (Map p.39)

This walk, on a good but rough path, through rocky moorland but not mountainous country, starts at Upper Toscaig, the most southerly village on the Applecross Peninsula (A). It is a matter of 'going there and coming back' by the same path so it can be made as long or as short as you like. The complete walk provides excellent views both of the Cuillin of Skye and of the mountain ranges south of Lochcarron.

For people staying at Torridon, Annat, Shieldaig or Lochcarron who would like to combine a round road trip of the Applecross Peninsula by car with some footwork it offers an ideal long day in fine summer weather. The whole trip is so beautiful it is, perhaps, a pity to waste it on a rainy day.

The best way round the peninsula by car is to go over the Bealach na Ba first (then that is over) and end the day touring the long coastal road back to Shieldaig in the late afternoon, when the Torridon mountains are magnificently floodlit by the late afternoon sun. In fact the Bealach road to Applecross is nowadays an easy undertaking for any experienced driver since the Z-bends have been considerably widened and barriers give protection against all steep edges. Park your car at the car park and viewpoint at the highest point (2,053 feet) and enjoy the magnificent views of the distant Cuillin (invisible in pouring rain). When cloud or mist are below 2,000 feet the drive over the

The road over the Bealach na Ba to Applecross.

Bealach can be unpleasant for the driver and even worse for the passenger, and is best avoided.

At Applecross turn left and continue south through Milton, Camusteel and Camusterrach, for 3½ miles, to Toscaig. Five yards before the TOSCAIG signpost (left-hand side) there is a hardstanding with room to park two or three cars if parked neatly. I suggest you leave your car there (A). (Upper Toscaig, where your walk begins, is an intimate cluster of cottages where you have to park your car on grass verges directly in front of somebody's house. If such niceties do not bother you the local inhabitants, being Highlanders, probably won't mind, but if you do decide to park in the village please do not do so in the turning lane at the end of the road.)

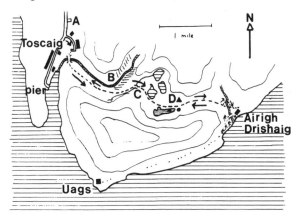

The walk from Upper Toscaig (A) to Airigh-drishaigh and back.
The highest point of the walk (860 feet) is at the cairn (D).

Walk down the road and turn left just before the signpost to Toscaig pier (worth a separate visit but less attractive than Upper Toscaig). At the upper end of the road in Upper Toscaig (714386) cross grassy lawns and the wooden bridge over the river. Then turn left, with power poles on your right. Shortly cross a burn, using the remains of a little wooden bridge and head SE uphill with the power poles 25 yards or so to your right. Almost immediately thereafter the path becomes clearly defined.

If a lot of unnecessary waffle irritates you all you need to do is to read the next sentence:- *Follow this path for 3¾ miles to Airigh-drishaig and return by the same route.* If, however, you find it helpful to have a

39

few targets to aim for on your way, read on:-

The worst parts of this path are the first 200 yards up rough broken stone and the last ½ mile down a smaller more muddy path. The rest, except in midwinter when it is largely out of reach of the very low winter sun and tends to be inconveniently iced in many parts, is excellent as mountain paths go. The minimum target should be the impressive gorge at the bend of the River Toscaig (B) 728375 (1¼ miles, 2½ miles return; ¾ hours to reach there, 1½ hours return). The view of the Cuillin over your shoulder will attract you but they will be the big feature in your return joùrney.

The next target (only a further ⅓ mile) is the wooden bridge over a delightful burn situated in a miniature valley surrounded by crags (C). The bridge is a good place to sit and eat some chocolate with your feet dangling over the water.

The path now winds uphill, through wilder country and past dramatically situated lochans and through a swing gate in an intact fence to a cairn marking its highest point (D) (860ft.) just beyond the 'dot' lochan of what I call the exclamation mark loch (actually Loch Airigh Alasdair (749371)).

As you approach this, lovely views of the mountains S of Loch Carron appear.

This is the moment for decision; whether to descend 800 feet and 1¼ miles to reach the coast and old cottage or to turn back. Only if you decide to proceed to the end, however, may you find the answer to the question, where are the power lines, which have been accompanying you throughout your walk, leading to? This final section takes about 1 hour 20 minutes there and back.

The path becomes narrower and descends fairly steeply until you reach a burn with small pools and falls which must be crossed. Athletes will wish to swing across on the rusty old wires which, presumably, mark the site of a previously more inviting form of crossing. The rest may prefer to use the ladder 25 yards upstream which is easy and safe; but both means of crossing are unconventional. Then it is plain sailing, if a bit rough, down to the wooded shore, the isolated cottage (please respect the owner's privacy), and the remains of earlier croft houses.

The views across to the Red Cuillin and to Plockton (hidden by its plock) and the entrance to Loch Carron are very fine and on a windless day the silence is broken only by the birds, the occasional boat far away on the sea loch and the constant chatter of the little water-wheel 15 yards from the cottage.

If you are using an old Ordnance Survey map you will notice a path marked on the map leading W to Uags. You will see the wooden bridge that led across the river to it but the path has now disappeared and has been deleted from the latest issue. It is difficult to imagine what it must have been like living in such remote places. A walk round the coast via Uags back to Toscaig is not recommended as it involves free-ranging 5½ miles over extremely rough country, crossing a seemingly endless series of promontories and valleys from 50-300 feet high. It should only be attempted by experienced hill walkers with a glutton for punishment. Far better to climb one of Torridon's fine mountains.

Walking back to Toscaig along the path one sees everything afresh travelling in the opposite direction, the last mile and a half being dominated by the fine views of Scalpay and the Cuillin dead ahead.

If you have time, visit Lower Toscaig and its pier and the little village of Aird-dubh in your car before returning to Applecross. From here take the fine coast road north. Until Cuaig the glories of this drive are the views of Raasay and Skye across the inner sound of the Minch. After Cuaig, the drive through Fearnmore, Arina, past Kenmore, and Ardheslaig to the Shieldaig road, is dominated by the gradually unfolding views of Loch Torridon and the Torridon mountains, on a fine day brilliantly floodlit by the late afternoon or evening sun.

Bealach na Ba - 'bealuhh-na-bar' - pass of the cattle.
Airigh-drishaig - 'ar-drisheg' - bay of the thorny shieling.
Toscaig - 'tosh-caig' - bay of the low strip.
Plock - promontory or peninsula.
Aird Dubh - 'Ar-doo' - black cliff or promontory.
Aig, Uig, Uag, Wick - are all derived from the Norse and mean bay.

Walks up into the Mountains

Walks 10 and 11 are suggested for anyone who, whilst not a mountain walker used to ascending mountain summits, would like to experience the wildness and roughness of high mountain places. These walks take one right under the summit cliffs of two great mountains, Beinn Eighe and Fuar Tholl, up good well-defined mountain paths, down which it is easy to find one's way back should mist develop. However, it is not recommended that they should be attempted in bad weather, nor under icy or snowy conditions in winter. Nor should inexperienced walkers decide suddenly to 'have a go for the top'. This should only be the intention of properly equipped and experienced mountaineers from the outset. Boots are essential and map and compass and extra clothing advised.

EW10: The Coire an Laoigh of Beinn Eighe. (Beinn Eighe Nature Reserve)

3 miles.   4.8km.   3-4 hours. Ascent 2,000 feet.
O.S. sheet 25. (Map p.89)

Beinn Eighe and Liathach are the two Torridonian giants which dominate the N side of the road from Kinlochewe to Torridon. An excellent but fairly steep path ascends to the Coire an Laoigh (the corrie, or hollow, of the calf) from the roadside at 977578 (A). This is 4¾ miles W from Kinlochewe and 1¼ miles E of the Glen Torridon car park.

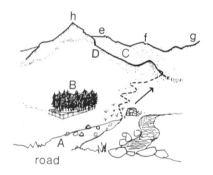

The place can be recognised from the road by the distinctive little oblong copse of pine trees standing 100 yards back from the roadside (B). Coming from Torridon there are places to park two cars at the entrance of a blocked up road quarry just *before* you reach the path or, if already occupied, ¼ mile beyond the path, both on the right side of the road. (The former has recently been unblocked but may be blocked up again.)

Simply follow the distinct path as it winds up steep ground into the

42

lower corrie. Only 100 yards of it are marshy at the beginning opposite the copse. When you reach the lower corrie the path fades out. Cross the stream and ascend into the upper main corrie on grass and easy sandstone slabs with the stream in a gorge on your right.

The corrie is a wild and impressive place with great scree slopes plunging down from the peaks above (from W to E; Spidean Coire nan Clach (3,188ft.), the peak of the stony corrie (e); Sgurr Ban, the white peak (f) and Sgurr nan Fhir Duibhe, the black peak of the old man (g)). Go to the edge of the small gorge down which the stream descends in small waterfalls. In the moist protected chasm beautiful varieties of mosses grow.

On your left are the grassy and rocky slopes of the smaller Stuc Coire an Laoigh (h), the shoulder (D) of which is easily attained from higher up the corrie and gives more dramatic views both of the corrie itself and of the mountains and of Loch Clair to the SW. (The Coire nan Clach is on the W side of this peak.) Unless you are really experienced on mountains please do not attempt to go higher on this peak, nor attempt to ascend the slopes at the head of the corrie leading to the ridge and thence to the summit of the Spidean Coire nan Clach. They are a lot steeper than they appear. Return to the road by the same path.

The scree slopes of Beinn Eighe (Sgurr an Fhir Duibhe) from high up in the Coire an Laoigh.

EW11: The Cold Hollow of Fuar Tholl (2,974 feet). (Commences at Achnashellach)

6 miles. 9.6km. 4-5 hours. Ascent 2,000 feet.
O.S. sheet 25. Wading may be necessary; take spare socks.

Fuar Tholl, the mountain whose easterly crags tower above Achnashellach station, means 'cold hollow' and it is from its high northern corrie, containing the famous and impressive Mainreachan buttress, which faces north, that it gets its name. This is a longer and more arduous expedition but there is a clearly defined path the whole way which is easily followed in mist. The cold hollow is a wild and desolate place and is well worth a visit if you have a taste for this sort of scenery, but do not attempt it in bad weather, snow or ice.

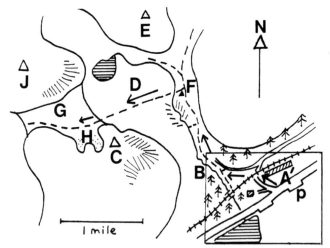

The long walk to the cold hollow of Fuar Tholl (H) from Achnashellach station (A). The area between (A) and (B) has been enlarged for clarity.

Park your car on the south side of the Achnasheen-Lochcarron road at the turning to Achnashellach station at (A) (005484). The B.R. sign is partly obscured by trees so keep a sharp look out for it. It is not permitted to take vehicles up the private road to the station. The problem with this walk is locating the beginning of the path. The smaller sketch plan shows you how to do it (A).

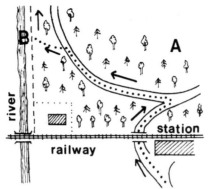

Cross the railway line by going through the two vehicular gates. Then follow the track uphill and to the right until you meet the main forest road. Turn sharp left where your track joins the main forestry track and proceed for ¼ mile until you come to the new gate across it. Pass through the pedestrian swing-gate portion and continue up the track for another 500m or so. A side path to your left then leads you through a new deer fence to the main mountain path.

The path now climbs steadily for the next 1¼ miles, and as you emerge from the trees the wild scenery, and particularly the crags of Fuar Tholl's buttresses (C), are most impressive. The path keeps away from the gorge of the River Lair to your left but it is well worth going up the little side path or, higher up, across rough grassy ground, to look down into it. As the path levels off you come into the vast and gloomy Coire Lair (D), with Beinn Liath Mhor (E) ahead and Sgorr Ruadh (J) to your left.

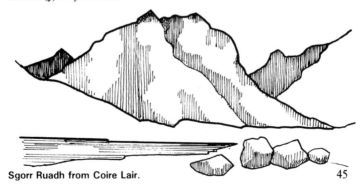

Sgorr Ruadh from Coire Lair.

45

Be alert for the cairn at about the highest point, which marks the smaller path going down to the river (F) (991502), and thence up to Fuar Tholl. Descend steeply and cross the river. The exact place where the path opposite reaches the river (or for 10 yards downstream) is the best place for crossing, so it is a waste of time working your way up and downstream looking for somewhere better. If the water is low you will be able to get across on the serrated (and therefore not slippery) rocks at the path end. If the water is higher wade a few yards further downstream (but do not take your boots off to do this otherwise you risk cutting your feet badly).

Once across (and socks changed) a good path will lead you, in 1½ miles, to the bealach (pass) (G) between Fuar Tholl and Sgorr Ruadh and across the mouth of the cold hollow (H). In the middle stands the magnificent Mainreachan buttress with screes on either side. The screes on the left side of the buttress are the way to the main summit but do not attempt these unless you are an experienced hill walker and had planned the full ascent from the outset.

The Mainreachan buttress in the cold hollow of Fuar Tholl.
S = main summit.

Before returning by the way you came it is worth continuing along to the path's end until you can see down into the next valley, but do not attempt a descent on this side. Across the valley are the ramparts of Meall na Ceapairean and Maol Chean Dearg. It is a gloomy place.

Shieldaig

LONG AND HIGH LEVEL WALKS

There are many fine walks to be enjoyed in Torridon, taking the walker into rough and wild areas, but the numerous excellent stalker's paths make a lot of the going easier. The walks I have chosen to describe keep below 2,000 feet, but full mountain gear (as you would carry for the ascent of high peaks) is advised as they will take you into remote places. Other than in exceptionally dry weather, boots are essential. In wet weather burns, hardly noticed in dry, may be difficult to cross and in full spate, dangerous. In the event of a crossing mishap, spare socks carried in the haversack can make life more comfortable. The distances quoted are approximate and do not account for altitude, the delights of ascending and descending being extra. The times suggested are based upon a person in reasonable training, going steady but not fast, and refer to the *total* walking time.

LONG AND HIGH LEVEL WALKS

COIRE MHIC FHEARCHAIR AND THE
CIRCUMNAVIGATION OF BEINN ALLIGIN
(O.S. sheets 19, and 25)

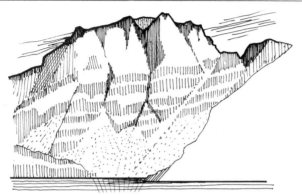

The great buttresses of Beinn Eighe dominate the Coire Mhic Fhearchair.

Most walkers know of the seven mile path which goes round the back
(north side) of Liathach. On the large scale O.S. 1:25,000 map it is
marked in bold green elongated dots, giving the impression that the
walk will be easy like a stroll in Kew Gardens. This is not so, and there
are two snags to it. Firstly, if you leave your car at one end, how do
you get back to it after you have completed that 7-8 mile slog?
Secondly, about two miles of the middle part are unpleasantly marshy
with up and down bogs and so forth. I therefore venture to suggest two
alternatives which still traverse the best parts of this rough track and
offer far greater rewards for the mountain lover, and incidentally bring
you back to your car.

W1: Walk to Coire Mhic Fhearchair

(Farquhar's son's Corrie or 'corrie -vik-errihher')
O.S sheets 25 and 19. Distance 7¹/₂ miles 12 km. Height 1,980ft.
Time 4¹/₂ hours. This walk is permitted throughout the stalking season.
(Map.50)
This splendid corrie is a special place for those who love wild scenery.
Containing a sizeable loch it is dominated at the far end by the famous
three buttresses of Beinn Eighe, on the left by Ruadh Stac Mor, the
mountain's highest peak and to the right by the forbidding Sail Mhor

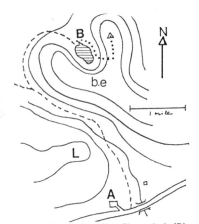

Walk to the Coire Mhic Fhearchair (B).
Leave your car at the Glen Torridon car park (A) (957568).
The path starts 15 yards down the road and goes up the Coire Dubh
Mhoir, between Liathach (L) and Beinn Eighe (be).

('Sail-vor, the great heel).

Leave your car in the car park at the head of Glen Torridon (957568). Walk a few yards along the road towards Kinlochewe. Just before crossing the bridge over the Allt a' Choire Dubh Mhoir ('Alt a' hhorry-doo-voor') pick up the obvious path ascending NW up the Coire Duhb Mor (which, lacking the h's of its river is pronounced 'corrie-doo-mor'). Now the fun begins. On your left the path is dominated by Liathach's most easterly peak the Stuc a' Choire Dubh Bhig (the peak of the small black hhorry) and to the right the impressive scree slopes of the ridge joining Beinn Eighe's Spidean Coire nan Clach (the peak of the stony corrie) to the great heel, Sail Mhor. Well up and into the corrie, which is really a valley, you have some big firm stepping stones to negotiate, and as you progress the track becomes more and more dominated by the massive northern precipices of Liathach. Two and a half miles up, just after a small reedy lochan to your right (and mercifully before the really squelchy part of the track commences) note, to your right, a cairn, and another, and another. Veer to the right (northwards), leaving the main track, over rock slabs and marshy ground following any of the two or three muddy rough paths which walkers have made in futile endeavours to avoid the worst of the swamps hereabouts. These alternatives gradu-ally resolve into a single rough track ascending, with some ups and

1998: A good path now leads to the coire.

downs, and winding round the NW aspect and cliffs of Sail Mhor. If you feel like cursing this bit, be assured that it is preferable to what would have followed if you had continued along the main path which you have just left.   Remember also that you are really going somewhere, the great Corrie itself.

Gloomy old Beinn a' Chearcaill comes into view and can disappoint you if you are tired and thinking it is Ruadh-stac Mor marking the far side of the corrie you are seeking. You have farther to go. But in due course you are rewarded as you ascend beside the cascading waterfalls from the corrie's loch, to your left, and with an easy struggle upwards you emerge on the flat slabs at the mouth of the corrie which now lies impressively before you, inviting you to linger and explore. In due course return by the way you came.

Ascent of Ruadh-stac Mor, Beinn Eighe's highest peak. 3,309ft.
For the determined and energetic the possibility of going to the summit, which is a taxing 1½ miles, 1,300ft. and 1-1½ hours away, presents itself. Should you decide to do this (not part of the recommended walk), make your way along the rough terrain on the left (NE) side of the loch nearly to the end of the corrie. A threatening scree gully presents ahead. Frustrate its implied evil intentions by ascending up the steep but easier scree, grass and boulder-ridden slopes on the left side somewhat before you reach the actual gully. Choose a part where there are most grassy patches and larger boulders to cling to as you ascend. These slopes are steep, but not dangerous, and just when you think the steepness will never relent, it does. When you reach the shoulder, note the place for when you come to descend, and turn northwards for the summit. At the summit nature has built a huge cairn of shattered quartzite boulders upon which man has erected a generous but puny one of his own. The view from this point across to the northern side of the Beinn Eighe massif is wild and very impressive.

If you decide to include the summit of Ruadh-stac Mor, your total expedition will take you 7-8 hours.

Man's little cairn, on top of nature's big one, on the summit of Ruadh-stac Mor.

W2: Walk Round Beinn Alligin.

O.S sheet 24. Distance 8 miles, 13km. Height 1,800ft. Time 4¹/₂-5 hours. You may do this walk during the stalking season. (Map p.53)

Retrospect of the north face of Liathach from the path round the Horns of Beinn Alligin.

The northern and western aspects of Beinn Alligin are even finer than the SE aspect, as seen from across Loch Torridon, which is familiar to every visitor to the region. Once you have walked round this mountain and, on another day, traversed its summits, you will feel you have come to know Beinn Alligin in a way that the high ridge traverse alone does not afford. Although rough in parts, this walk is a delight all the way and I strongly recommend it.

Leave your car at the Beinn Alligin car park on the Torridon/ Diabaig road (869576). Ascend the excellent path up the Coire Mhic Nobuil ('corry-vic-nobul') beside the dramatic tumbling water of the Abhainn Coire Mhic Nobuil, to your right the slopes of Sgorr a' Chadail, Liathach's most westerly peak. As you ascend, the impressive SE face of Beinn Alligin becomes progressively more visible and you can see up into the corrie which is the easiest route to the summit of Tom na Gruagaich, the most southerly peak of Beinn Alligin. After a mile cross the river by a sturdy wooden bridge and head due north up the even rougher track towards the Alligin Horns. After 200 yards note the cairn marking the continuation of the main track going behind (north of) Liathach to your right. After a further half mile of uphill work, you cross another wooden bridge in a delightful hollow. From now on the path becomes progressively rougher and more indis-

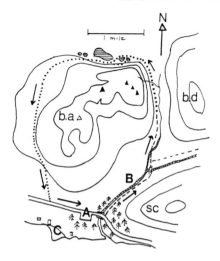

Walk round Beinn Alligin.
Alligin car park (A), Coire Mhic Nobuil (B), Rechullin (East Inveralligin) (C)
Beinn Alligin (ba), Beinn Dearg (bd), Sgorr a' Chadail (sc).

tinct as you come under the impressive Horns of Alligin to your left, and you will pass a cluster of cairns on rocky platforms marking the usual route of ascent up the Horns. Do not fuss, it matters little if you lose the path, for the going is better, and from now on throughout this walk you simply stay close to the cliffs and steep slopes of the mountain always on your left. As you ascend the pass between the Horns and Beinn Dearg (the Bealach a' Chomhla) the impressive southern slopes of Baosbheinn ('Bersh-ven') come more and more into view.

At the head of the pass, cross a wide but easily negotiated waterfall (but I have not seen it in spate). Immediately ascend rough steep ground to your left (E) beside the waterfall. As you round the Horns and come under their dramatic N precipices you are likely to find yourself passing to the N of the first two small lochans, but go to the S (close to the mountain) of the much larger Loch Toll nam Biast and the two small lochans to the W of it, as the ground to the N of this loch tends to be swampy. As you continue round the impressive cliffs of Sgurr Mhor you may be surprised (if you have not previously studied the map carefully) to find these giving way to grass slopes leading to the summit. These offer an easy and almost direct route to the summit but it is better to go to the lowest point of the ridge first. That summit is, in fact, 1,400 feet and half a mile away, and its ascent is not part of this walk; but if you feel tempted...At least note that these slopes offer a convenient escape route off the mountain's northern side. As you progress you will pass the impressively wild unnamed corrie beneath Tom na Gruagaich's ridge.

Continue for 1½ miles round the eastern slopes of the Tom, 'pick up' an old deer fence on your right and follow it round to about its lowest point (853590). Do not be drawn up again onto the crags on the southern aspect of the Tom. Below you, and due south, you will notice the bright green expanse of fields on the little peninsula at the eastern end of the village of Rechullin (E. Inveralligin) - 857573. If you now aim towards the road in the general direction of this attractive green patch you will be led down the easiest slopes to the S of Beinn Alligin to reach the road ¾ mile distant. You have my permission to curse the last 400 yards of rough marshy ground before you reach the road and, indeed, one's arrival at the road and the ½ mile walk down it back to your car come as a blessing after it. Open the boot of your car, take out your thermos of hot tea and congratulate yourself on a good day out while you drink it.

This is a rough and, in places, marshy but very stimulating walk and can be enjoyed in the stalking season providing you keep on the south side of Loch Toll nam Biast and keep close to Beinn Alligin on its western aspect.

W3: An Staonach-An Fur Ridge

O.S sheet 24. Distance 6-7 miles, 10-11km. Height 1,692ft. Time 4-5 hours. This walk is planned from the village of Shieldaig, and no car is required from this point. (Map p.56)

This is the broad ridge, facing Beinn Shieldaig, which runs along the SW side of Glen Shieldaig. Should the ridge appear to you somewhat gloomy from the glen it nevertheless offers splendid walking along its top and very fine views of its surrounding larger companions. The ridge is easily attained and can offer a delightful snow walk in suitable winter conditions.

Start the ascent of An Staonach (the stony place), 1,692ft. (830480) from the Shielding/Kishorn road at M.S.(851477). To reach this point, take Duncan MacLennan's white minibus from Shieldaig Post Box (daily at10.25 am. except Sunday, check up-to-date times) and ask him to put you down just before the vehicle track to Ceann Loch Damh

Shieldaig village

('Kinloch dam') at the head of Glen Shieldaig (there will be a charge for this service). Read your map and make a bee-line for An Staonach ascending up steep heather-covered slopes towards rocky outcrops direct from the road. The walking starts marshy but gets better the higher you go. It matters little precisely how you proceed. You will see or pass by two or three lochans and traverse two delightful mini-canyons with ease. The main slopes leading to the summit of An Staonach will appear before you, and its horizon ridge (not the summit) is more quickly reached than at first appears likely. In general, keep somewhat to the left (W) to avoid the steeper slopes and rocky buttresses to the right (E). When you reach the crest, you feel you are now on a mountain but the summit is still $\frac{1}{2}$ mile further on. Aim for it keeping always somewhat to the left rather than the right, where a false summit at first beckons seductively.

In due course, you may see, if it is still there, a stone finger pointing skywards and directing you towards the summit cairn. This small marker cairn was placed there by myself, as I like to have just one personal cairn in the region (although a Scottish climbing friend of mine detests the things and kicks them down).

The An Staonach ridge from Beinn Shieldaig.
Summit (s). Beinn Bhan is seen in the background.

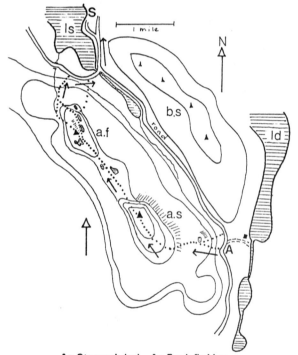

An Staonach (as) - An Fur (af) ridge.
Beinn Sheildaig (bs), Shieldaig village (S), Loch Shieldaig (ls),
Loch Damh (ld). The walk starts by going up the steep grass slopes (A)
above the road opposite the track to Ceann Loch Damh.

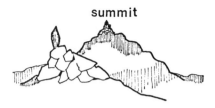

summit

From the summit of An Staonach, you obtain the very best views of the great corries of Beinn Bhan and ahead of you lies the ridge extending north to An Fur (the windy place) (808507),with Loch Lundie to the left. An Fur itself (1,257ft.) is obscured by two intermediate summits marked as 406m on the map. As you descend from An Staonach keep always somewhat to the left (W) rather than to the right in order to avoid its north-east rock buttresses. Descend to a large lochan at the lowest point on the ridge. Find your way along the very broad ridge past two more lochans. Should you desire to take in the two intermediate summits, be warned that there is a steepish descent on the farther (north) side.

At the foot of An Fur sprawls the large Lochan Prapa. Pass beyond it (to the right or left) to reach the summit of An Fur.

The easiest, but somewhat rough, descent from An Fur to the road is via a long grassy couloir (see p.58). Continue NW along the ridge for ¹⁄₂ mile and then descend to gain the top of this broad shallow valley. Follow the burn (An Garbh Allt), but cross it and keep to the right, close to crags, going over a small promontory to re-join the downward continuation of this valley. A fenced native woodland regeneration area now lies between you and the road. Aim towards the head of Loch Shieldaig (Ceann locha), ignoring small diversions of the couloir leading away to the left and you will come to a high stile, visible from higher up, by which you can climb over the fence (811522). An exit stile to the road lies ¹⁄₄ mile below diagonally to the L at the foot of the stream (812527). (There are four other stiles to the E which may be used for other walks). The estate owners are happy for walkers to cross this area to reach the road. Please respect the trees and flora, do not damage the fence by attempting to climb it other than by the stiles and note that deer management may be taking place at any time throughout the year in this area.

The fence extends NW as far as 803527 and can be avoided altogether if you prefer to continue NW along the ridge before descending to the road ¹⁄₄ mile S of Doire aonar (O.S.)

To extend the native woodlands, more extensive protective fencing is likely to be erected in 1999, with strategically placed stiles which walkers may use.

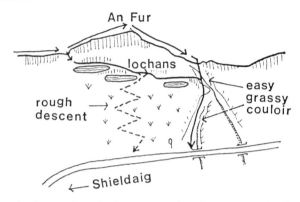

An easier descent from An Fur (—), avoiding the steep marshy slopes below its summit (---), takes advantage of the more gently sloping grassy couloir or hollow, ½ mile beyond (N).

W4: The Great Corries of Beinn Bhan

O.S sheet 24. Distance 6 (10) miles 9.7 (16)km. Height 1,300ft Time 4 (6) hours. (Map.59)

In the same way that the walk around Beinn Alligin, as well as its ascent, provides a fuller understanding of its topography, so does a visit to the magnificent corries of Beinn Bhan and an ascent of its summit help one to understand its massive shape and structure.

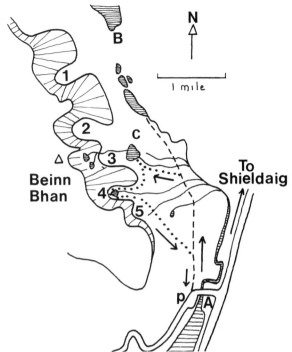

A walk to the great corries of Beinn Bhan.
(1,2,3,4,5) from Tornapress (A).------- stalker's path.
. . . . suggested route, over rough steep ground. (B) = Loch Lundie.
Car park (p). C = Lochan Coire na Poite.

The starting point for this walk is the ample parking space at Torna-press, half a mile up the road to Applecross (via the Bealach na Ba, the pass of the cattle) after it leaves the main Shieldaig to Kishorn road. The park is situated at 834423 just across the estuary. Leave your car here. Take the stalker's path (which is marked on the map) going N in the general direction of Loch Lundie and proceed for 2-3 miles. The five great corries now face you on your left. From N to S they are:

1. Unnamed (and most northerly).
2. Coire nan Fhamhair.
3. Coire na Poite (the cauldron).
4. Coire na Feola (the corrie of flesh).
5. Coire Each (corrie of the horse).

It is up to you to decide how big a day you wish to make of it, ie. whether you wish to visit all five corries (six hours) or just the three nearest ones (four hours). The ground is rough and you will ascend 1,000ft. The modest choice is to ignore corrie number one and ascend directly to the Lochan Coire na Poite (C). From there one can gaze up at the forbidding precipices of this corrie (you will be looking down here when you climb Beinn Bhan) and have a fair, if oblique, view of Corrie nam Fhamhair. Thence walk S round the impressive buttress of rock to ascend and enter the beautiful Coire na Feola which, in contrast, seems to welcome intruders. It is worth ascending deep up into this welcoming corrie, before re-descending to continue the walk. After enjoying the beauties of this corrie, descend obliquely SE to rejoin the stalker's path which will lead you back to the car park. And what of the Coire Each? Well, that is really only a dent in the mountain side.

W5: Walk round Beinn na h'Eaglaise (Annat-Drochaid Coire Roill).

O.S. sheets 24/25. Distance 7 miles, 11.3km. Height 1,250ft.
Time 4¹/₂-5 hours. Warning- difficult river crossings when in spate.
(Map p.61)

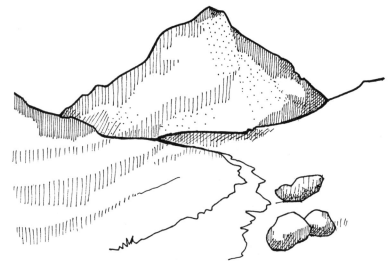

Maol Chean Dearg from the Annat path.

Let me be honest about the two snags involved in this otherwise delightful walk which, among other splendours, reveals Beinn Damh to be a much finer mountain than it appears from the road. Firstly, the walk annoyingly bestraddles the margins of two Ordnance Survey sheets. Secondly, it involves four river crossings which you will hardly fail to notice when the weather has been wet. In spate, either choose another walk or be prepared to use your ingenuity and carry spare socks. On the credit side, this walk uses excellent stalker's paths for all but one mile of its length and takes the walker deep into the south Torridon wilderness.

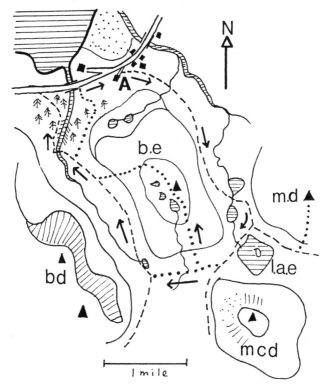

**The walk round Beinn na h-Eaglaise (be) begins at Annat (A).
Meall Dearg (md), Maol Chean Dearg (mcd), Beinn Damh (bd),
Loch an Eion (lae).**

Park your car just before Annat on the Shieldaig to Torridon road (894544). There is a convenient area on the left-hand side beside Loch Torridon just before the little house built into the rock face. The path (shown on the O.S. map) commences just east of the Torridon East Lodge House. Follow this excellent path eastwards, steadily ascending as it winds round the northern flank of Beinn na h-Eaglaise ('Ben-na-uggalish' - the mountain of the church) and off sheet 24 onto sheet 25. As you ascend, the views of Glen Torridon get better and better. After one mile, cross your first burn. If the plank bridge is still down, make for the gravel banks 20 yards downstream to your left where the crossing is easy. If any very timid soul finds this first river crossing taxing I advise that he or she considers giving up at this point, for it is the easiest by far of the four. One up, three to go (excluding trivia), but this one is the easiest, and in dry weather you will hardly notice it. As the path continues for the next mile and a half the view becomes dominated by the unfriendly looking Maol Chean Dearg ahead with the precipices of Beinn na h-Eaglaise to your right. The path now enters a vast amphitheatre of rock terraces and the going is good. Cross water obstacle number two by the large irregular stepping stones. I guess the manoeuvre is always possible, but more exciting when in spate. If these stepping stones are wet or icy it is safer to wade. This little river joins the Lochan Domhain with Loch an Uilt-bheithe.

Continue to the lovely Loch an Eion (loch of the bird). Note the path going left (E) to the Bealach na Lice ('Bealahh na Lihh' - pass of the flat stone). If your last river crossing has been bad (which will only be so if the water was torrential) consider changing your plans, if the thought of more rushing waters disconcerts you, by ascending the Bealach na Lice and then free-ranging to the summit cairn of Meall Dearg ('Mell-jerrag' - the red hill) then returning whence you came. If not, keep on the path and make your next river crossing (joining Loch an Eion with Lochan Domhain). Here the stepping stones are larger and more uneven. Three up, one to go! Ascend for ¼ mile beyond the Loch an Eion. Choose a suitable place to cross the some-what marshy ground and negotiate the odd peat bog to gain the grassy and boulder-strewn southern slopes of Beinn na h'Eaglaise. One mile of rough going, keeping to the lower slopes and going almost due W will bring you to the Kinloch Damh - Annat path as it enters the Drochaid Coire Roill (the bridge of the Corrie Roill). This path will eventually bring you back to the road just above the Loch Torridon Hotel.

Those who want more adventure and are equipped for a bit of

Maol Chean Dearg from the lochan of the Drochaid Coire Roill.

mountaineering, may prefer to climb to the top of Beinn na h'Eaglaise (which is included in the mountain ascents as it is over 2,000ft.), and go N along its broad delightful crest and descend W down rough, but easy, slopes to rejoin the path.

Otherwise keep to the path going NNW past the delightful lozenge-shaped lochan of the drochaid (do not fail to turn for a retrospective view of Maol Chean Dearg which, in calm weather, is beautifully reflected in the lochan, like a Chinese painting, and of the splendid array of peaks to the SW:- An Ruadh-stac, Maol Chean Dearg, Sgorr Ruadh, and Beinn Liath Mhor).

Continue N on this excellent path and back onto O.S. sheet 24. For the next mile and a half the walk is dominated by the magnificent precipices of Beinn Damh on your left. Crossing flat slabs of sandstone and insignificant burns, after 1½ miles the path begins to descend. Note an old deer fence to your right; it will lead you to an alternative way back to the road if you do not fancy the next and last water crossing, the allt (river) feeding the dramatic sixty foot waterfall further down. The path leads to a deep gorge where perhaps a bridge once stood. Come back a few yards and follow the little alternative path 15 yards upstream which will lead you to the favoured crossing place. The snag here is that there is a central rounded stone round which the water cascades that you have to step boldly onto! It is usually above water, but in torrent it becomes covered and being wet and with the vigorous movement of the water over it, a slip could result in an unpleasant fall. If you don't fancy it, I suggest you take one of two alternatives. Either go further upstream and simply wade across the broad pebbly bottom and get your feet wet (you only have ½ hour or so to go) or retrace your steps up the path about 200 yards to the broken deer fence. Follow this fence east across rough ground for ¼ mile and then proceed north downwards where the trees are thinnest, finding your way down the steep bracken-covered slopes to the track and thence the road just east of the river and road bridge crossing it. Careful map reading will help you to achieve this.

If, however, you have made your last crossing successfully, you can now enjoy the walk descending to the left of the river in the pine and rhododendron forest to the road. Shortly after you have entered the wood, by a group of big boulders, there is a small clearing which affords an excellent view of Beinn Damh's impressive waterfall. Once you reach the road you have half a mile walk back to your car at Annat.

This walk can, of course, be done in the opposite direction. However, it is over this last crossing that you are most likely to have to get your feet wet by wading, which seems to be a better thing to happen near the end rather than at the beginning of a day's walk, and if you come round clockwise as I have suggested and high waters make this last crossing difficult, you have the alternative escape route which I have described.

After a lot of rain (because of the river crossings) and in snowy conditions this walk constitutes a small adventure; in dry conditions it is a doddle.

W6: Walk to Applecross or Around Croic Bheinn

O.S. Sheet 24. Distance 9-10 miles 14.5-16km. Height 855ft.
(Croic Bheinn 1,626ft.). Time 4¹/₂-5 hours. (Map p.65).

A delightful path runs from Kenmore (754576) to Applecross (710445). An irritatingly rough path and track from Inverbain (787549) joins this path at 748492. If you can find some way of leaving your car at Kenmore and arrange for a lift back from Applecross, or vice versa, I cannot recommend the former path too strongly. Leave your car at the tiny car park above *Kenmore* (754576). The commencement of this path has been obliterated during the construction of the

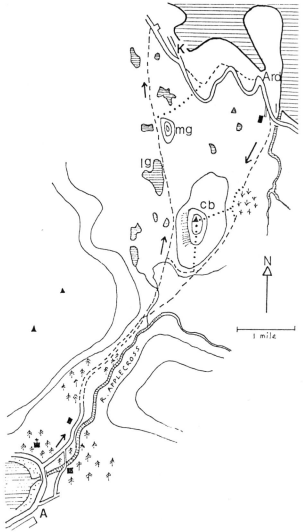

The walk from Applecross (A) to Kenmore (K) or vice versa or round Croic Bheinn (cb). Loch Gaineamhach (lg), Meall Dearg (mg), Ardheslaig (Ard), Inverbain (I).

Croic Beinn dominates the Kenmore to Applecross path.

new Shieldaig-Applecross coast road. Just aim SW up the rough ground beside the road and in 50 yards or so you will find it. Follow it all the way to Applecross (you end up walking along the road through the estate), past lochans including the lovely Loch Gaineamhach, the sandy loch, one third of the way, and under the impressive precipices of Croic Bheinn ('Crik-ven', the antler mountain) to your left; and finally down the long valley dominated by the steep slopes of Meall an Doireachan and Beinn a' Chlachain on the right. Keep your eyes skinned for deer for this is a major deer reserve. Unfortunately, the deer keep a very low profile in summer, but during the winter when the snow drives them down to lower ground you may see them in hundreds. This walk (approximately 10 miles to Applecross village and inn) is equally fine done in the opposite direction. Find out at Shieldaig or Applecross Post Office if you can get the necessary lift one way on the post bus.

If such arrangements do not seem possible, I recommend the following alternative. Leave your car at Inverbain (P). Just across the bridge over the Allt an t-Strathain (786548) a tiny path diagonals backwards, within the small copse. Alternatively take the main track (signposted as a right of way) a little farther up the road to and past the house.

This path must have been an old main track across the peninsula since it widens and becomes uncomfortable walking as you seem to be traversing its rough rocky foundations, well lubricated by water, and marshy ground on either side encourages one to grit one's teeth and

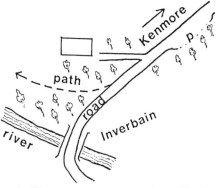

keep to the track. There are two compensations. Firstly, the fine view of the splendid falls of the Abhainn Dubh (the black river) on the opposite side of the valley; secondly the knowledge that your walk back on the other side of Croic Bheinn will be as delightful underfoot as this part can be irritating. The track becomes more of a path and as you approach Croic Bheinn leads you into wet, often flooded, grassy marshland and demands you to sort yourself out. Simple; just work your way through bracken round the higher ground of the E slopes of Croic Bheinn to your right. The occasional desultory cairn will signal you back to the path again which, from now on as you ascend, gets better and better. Now is your chance to take in the flat top summit of Croic Bheinn (1,626ft.) if you feel like climbing ½ mile and a mere 650ft. of easy slopes, to rejoin your path or the path running behind (S) of Croic Bheinn linking the main Inverbain-Applecross and Kenmore-Applecross tracks. From now on the going N is excellent. As you pass Loch Gaineamhach on your left, you will be considering the fact that the path is taking you to Kenmore whereas your car and that thermos of hot tea are at Inverbain. So, as you pass little Meall Dearg (the red hill, 920ft.) on your right, choose a good moment to short cut 3 miles by making a direct cross-country bee-line in a NE direction to the road, passing S of Loch a' Choire Bhuidhe ('Lohh a' hhorrie-bui', the loch of the yellow corrie). The walk back to Inverbain along the road is lovely, with views of the Torridon mountains floodlit by the afternoon or evening sun when it feels like obliging. Picking up the old coastal track, clearly marked on the map and visible to the naked eye, adds interest and subtracts another ½ mile from your walk. Those who opted against going to the summit of Croic Bheinn will surely wish to ascend the little slopes of Meall Dearg instead, and by going straight (NE) over the top and down to the road will shorten their walk by yet a further ½ mile.

W7:   Heights of Kinlochewe and Gleann Bianasdail

O.S. sheet 19. Distance 14 or 10 miles 22.5 or 16km. Height approx. 1,000ft Time 8 or 7 hours. (Map p.69)
Avoid this walk during the stalking season. Shooting takes place on this estate from mid-August to February.

The graceful appearance of Slioch's easterly peak (Sgurr an Tuill Bhain) from above the Heights of Kinlochewe.

This area is outside the Torridon region, as defined in my introduction, but immediately adjacent to it, and, along with the ascent of Slioch (see p.98), is too good not to be included.

Beyond and to the N of Loch Maree lies the wild mountainous region of the Fisherfield Forest (no trees) and this walk gives a glimpse of it across the splendid Lochan Fada (the long lochan). Consult your O.S. sheet 19 and you will find the area under consideration lying immediately to the N of Kinlochewe (026619). The walk I propose is circular and 13-14 miles long, not including ascents and descents, but allowing for twists and turns in the paths. It involves unavoidably wading across a shallow 20ft. wide river with a hard pebble and rock bed and 1¾ miles of free-ranging across rough ground. It can, of course, be made in either direction, clockwise or anti-clockwise, and is spectacular throughout. On the assumption that, like myself, you prefer the adventure first and a nice easy stroll downhill on a good track at the end of the day, I will describe the clockwise direction,

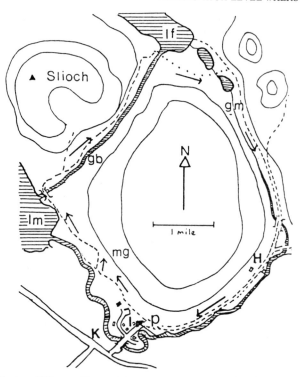

Walk round Gleann Bianasdial (gb) and the Heights of Kinlochchewe (H). Kinlochewe (K), Incheril (I), parking (p), Loch Maree (lm), Meallan Ghobhar (mg), Lochan Fada, Gleann na Muice (gm).

starting at Incheril (035621) 1 mile E of Kinlochewe, traversing up Gleann Bianasdail to the head of Lochan Fada and returning via Gleann na Muice and the Heights of Kinlochewe. Should you prefer a shorter walk in this area, you can alternatively go up Gleann Bianasdail to the point at which you have a good view of Lochan Fada and A' Mhaighdean ('A'Vuhhvayn', the maiden), Beinn Tarsuin and the Mullach Coire Mhic Fhearchair, thence returning by the same route which is exciting enough easily to bear the repeat journey. Easiest of all, particularly in winter snow, is to walk up the good track to the right (ENE) from Incheril to the Heights of Kinlochewe and beyond as far, say, as Loch Gleann na Muice (062686) - good path all the way - when

69

you will discover why Slioch is called 'the spear', (alternatively 'sliabhach' - place of slopes) because of the shape of its westerly peak, Sgurr an Tuill Bhan, and possibly taking in the broad rocky and grassy little summit of Meallan Odhar (071677) for better views of the Fisherfield giants to the NW.

Park your car in the large signposted car park in Incheril and 'pick up' the adjacent track running NW at the foot of the slopes of Meallan Ghobhar ('Mellen-gova', the goat hill). After 1½ miles (45 minutes) of delightful walking, with the Kinlochewe river on your left, look assiduously for a stone-built arrow embedded in grassy ground to the right of the path you are on.

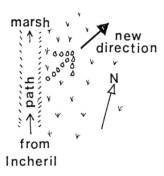

If you continue to follow what seems to be the main path, you will end up splashing around in the shallow overflow waters of the river along with the ducks and sheep. Follow the direction of the arrow across a flat grassy meadow and the path you should be taking defines itself again. This path now leads you right down to Loch Maree's edge, through a wilderness of dead tree trunks and natural debris, and then across open ground to a fine bridge which allows you to cross the tumbling waters of the Abhainn an Fhasaigh, the river running down the length of Gleann Bianasdail from Lochan Fada to Loch Maree, which is to be your companion for the next 3 miles. Take the path immediately right over the bridge. This comes a bit close to the edge of the river gorge at one point; OK when dry, but if wet and slippery or particularly if iced, it could deliver you into the gorge below. If you wish to avoid this, follow the path straight ahead up a bracken-covered slope and veer again to the right and pick up your original path again. You are now crossing marshy ground and the path is vague in places, but keep travelling NE. Note a cairn marking the marshy path to your left, which is the lead off for climbing Slioch.

Half a mile further on the path once again comes very close to the gorge edge: again OK when dry but if iced it is safer simply to free-range up the grass and bracken slope straight ahead, rejoining the path beyond this short stretch of narrows, thus thwarting the path's attempts to give you a minor scare. From now on, all is plain sailing up the wild but friendly Gleann Bianasdail to its highest point and then zig-zagging gently down to the mouth of the Abhainn.

Now for the rough bit. Ford the wide but shallow river, and for those who have got them, empty your boots of water and change your socks. Set your compass ESE in order to cross the 1½ miles of flattish rough country to join up with the path which will lead you south to the Heights of Kinlochewe and back to Incheril, crossing either between Loch an Sgeireach and Loch Gleann na Muice (056689) or just south of the latter. Proceed down an ever-improving track, down the splendid valleys of Gleann na Muice and the Heights of Kinlochewe with its well-kept farmhouse and scattered uninhabited cottages. I have recommended a clockwise direction for this walk but the views of the mountains beyond Lochan Fada and down to Loch Maree are better if you prefer to ascend the heights of Kinlochewe first going in an anticlockwise direction. *Avoid making this crossing entirely during the stalking and shooting season. (Mid-August to February.)*

W8: An Sgurr (Kishorn)

O.S sheet 24. Distance 4 miles, 6.4km. Height 1,293ft. Time 3 hours. (Map p.72). Avoid this walk in the stalking season.

Two local humps provide half-day walks with good tops and good views, An Sgurr above Kishorn (857387), and Seana Mheallan which forms the south wall of Glen Torridon.

For An Sgurr take your car to Kishorn and turn down the road to Ardarroch and Achintraid (840388). Leave your car beside the road before Achintraid (just before the bridge on the left is a good spot), unless you particularly like parking your car right outside somebody else's cottage. Walk into Achintraid and go up the broad track between houses and a farm, left; (path goes SE) marked on the O.S. map (840388). Ignore the barking dogs and flapping geese and ascend,

An Sgurr from Ardarroch (Kishorn).

passing through a gate and then up by a plantation on your left. After ½ mile the track curves sharply up to the right. *Carry on straight forward* at this point with the plantation fence close to your left. As you approach a mound ahead follow the track (and/or tractor tracks) curving to the right over its crest. (Leaving the main path at this point

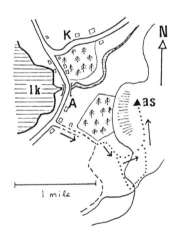

An Sgurr (as), Achintraid (A), Kishorn (K), Loch Kishorn (lk).

reduces substantially the amount of marshy ground you must traverse to reach your little mountain.) Take a direction ESE with A Sgurr's crags above you, ascending rising ground, eventually to link up with the fence again, which will lead you to hitherto concealed gate (the gate and the post surprisingly both turn as you open it). You are now below a break in the crags (853378), and can ascend the mountain up an easy but steep slope. Once on the plateau you can enjoy exploring and discovering which is the (cairned) true summit, ascending or circumnavigating various ridges which put up mock defences to bar your way. The true summit is more to your right than you are likely to suspect as you ascend. From the summit there are excellent views, particularly of the Cuillin of Skye. This ascent can be recommended under snow conditions in winter, being only of modest altitude, but in mist, without a compass, you could become totally confused when trying to get off the summit. (At the time or writing a new (presumed temporary) deer fence blocks the way to the actual summit.)

Return the way you ascended (easily missed if you have not taken due notice during your ascent). In mist, or if you prefer, proceed *due south from the summit* until you meet the little burn at 857377, which will lead you comfortably down between the two buttresses of crags on An Sgurr's westerly aspect. This is a fine high plateau and you can alternatively turn it into a full day's outing by going NE from the summit to Loch a Choire Leith (loch of the grey corrie) and thence due north to join the Lochcarron to Kishorn road, but this diversion will add a further 4-5 miles to your walk and the going is somewhat rough and marshy. At all times keep a lookout for deer which favour this little-visited region.

W9: Seana Mheallan (Glen Torridon)

O.S sheet 25. Distance 5 miles 8km. Height 1,380ft. Time 3 hours.

When driving down Glen Torridon towards Shieldaig one's eyes are ever drawn by the mighty southern precipices of Liathach, so that one hardly takes notice of the somewhat gloomy looking and comparitively insignificant lump which is Seana Mheallan ('Shen-vellen', the old hill) on the other side (south) of the glen. Yet this is a fine broad topped elevation which offers an excellent morning or afternoon's walk with fine views, and the best of Liathach's famous pinnacles, an Fasarinen. The rivers Torridon and Thrail, which mark its N, W and S boundaries, have to be waded except in unusually dry weather and can be dangerous to cross in spate. The bridge implied by the continuation of a dotted path at 919539 is defunct and the ground all round the Abhainn Thrail is unpleasantly marshy. I therefore suggest you approach and return from the hill's *eastern* flanks. The walk is 90 per cent free-ranging and is a good way of finding out if you wish to climb the larger Torridon peaks which do not have paths up them, which are the majority, as the ground you will cover on this walk is similar.

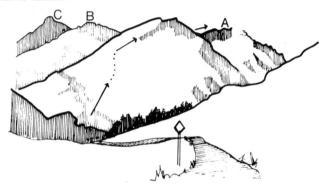

Seana Mheallan, seen from the road to Glen Torridon.
(A) summit, (B) Beinn na h'Eaglaise, (C) Beinn Damh.
The arrows indicate the recommended route of ascent and descent,
from the Ling path on the east side.

Park your car at the car park at the head of Glen Torridon (958568) and walk east down the road for 100 yards, turning right (south) up the excellent stalker's path which passes by the Ling (climber's) Hut which is marked on the O.S. map. Ascend by the waterfall of the unnnamed burn which runs into the Lochan an Lasgair. After ¾ mile you cross a stream. Somewhere between this and the next stream crossing look down to your right for the obvious gravel banks in the main burn you are following. Veer off WSW, descending heather banks, to cross the stream and head almost due W up easy slopes (circumventing occasional miniature canyons) towards Seanna Mheallan's summit. In the lower part the going is marshy but things get better and better as you ascend. The first 'summit' on your horizon is, of course, the usual fool's gold, but this will lead you on to a huge gently inclined slab of sandstone on which stands a giant's dining table and seat; on the top of the former rock stands a small cairn. For all its magnificence, this is not the summit which is a

74

further ½ mile on. You are now among a series of delightful chasms and lochans and surrounded by Seana Mheallan's bigger neighbours.

The true summit cairn is dramatically placed on the great sloping buttress of rock which affords magnificent views up Loch Torridon. You will surely want to explore this broad top with its numerous lochans before returning. Those who wish to swim the Abhainn Thrail may descend SW (to avoid the westerly and north-westerly crags) and trudge all the way back up the road up Glen Torridon to their cars with squelching feet. Others, like myself, will prefer to turn back east visiting lochans and descending down easy slopes to rejoin the Ling Hut path. Do not undertake this walk during the stalking season without permission.

W10:   Three Flowerdale Miniatures; Meall a' Ghlas Leothaid, Meille na Meine and Meall Lochan a' Chleirich.

O.S.. sheet 19.   Distance 7-8 miles 11-13km. Height 1,384ft. Time 4-6 hours. (Map p.77)

The Flowerdale Valley belies its name. It is a rough and wild place. Three miniature mountains are grouped together and offer an opportunity for playing at mountaineering when you don't feel up to the big stuff; nevertheless, if you traverse all three of them you will have climbed, in total, 2,200 feet, but in easy stages. I recommend this hill walk, among wild and impressive scenery, either on a fine day or, as a little adventure, on a rough one when the big summits are best left alone. The wildness of the scene is augmented by the presence of the adjacent giants, Boasbheinn and Beinn an Eoin and in the distance Slioch and the Letterewe mountains. Essentially this is a day for finding one's own way up and down these individual craggy and grassy prominences, so I will not insult you with detailed routes. However, extensive recent afforestation is likely, in time, to make it difficult to reach the flanks of these little mountains from the track which leads ultimately to Loch na h-Oidche; but this track has been upgraded and can be entered by new access gates at each end of the planted area. When climbing these 'miniatures' has become impracticable, the track can be still used for the long walk to the loch, or the ascent of Beinn an Eoin and Baosbheinn (see map on p.105). The fun is in negotiating the miniature cliffs and buttresses, but a few comments will not be amiss.

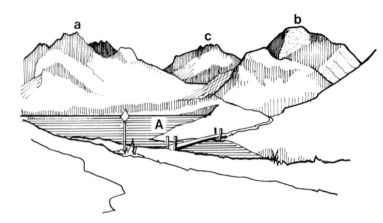

Three Flowerdale Miniatures, Meall Lochan a' Chleirich (a), Meall a' Ghlas Leothaid (b), and Meall na Meine (c), and the path by Am Feur Loch (A) leading to them. The path also leads to Loch na h-Oidhche, Baosbheinn and Beinn an Eoin.

Park your car by the corrugated iron barn on the Kinlochewe to Gairloch road, just beyond Am Feur Loch (a windy loch) at 857721. There is room for 3 or 4 cars. Take the track which commences on the opposite side of the road, after crossing the wooden bridge, and goes SE all the way to Loch na h-Oidhche ('loch-na-h'oihh', loch of night) beyond. This is a broad track, stony and rough and *if you simply want a walk* I can recommend a stroll to the loch and back (total 8½ The track is so definite and wide that it can take you into the heart of the wildest scenery in perfect safety except in the harshest winter conditions, when nothing is safe. The gorge of the Abhainn a' Gharbh Choire ('Avain- a garve-hhorry', the river of the rough corrie) is dramatic, and you will have fun going over the steeping stones at 886676 if they are wet (it is easier to cross fifteen yards upstream to the right as you approach using the little island where the burn divides). A Nissen hut (left open; but replace the wooden door peg when you leave) offers shelter against driving hail and sleet at the head of the loch.

Back then to the little mountains. I suggest an anti-clockwise route, climbing *Meall a' Ghlas Leothaid* ('mel a' glass-leohh', the hill of the

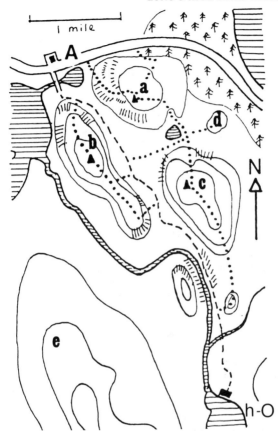

Three Flowerdale Miniatures.
Meall Lochan a' Chleirich (a), Meall a' Ghlas Leothaid (b), and Meille
na Meine (c). Meall nan Bacan (d), Am Feur loch (A), Baosbheinn (e)
--------- path   .... suggested routes. Loch na h-Oidche (h-O)

grey slope) first. The northern buttresses look daunting but you can
easily find a way up them to reach the cairned summit. Like Beinn
Damh this peak has its own 'lady peak' to the SE and you can keep
on the high ground to reach this. The gloomy appearance of Baosbheinn will attract your attention. The extreme south end of this
daughter prominence has buttresses, but there is a grass slope at the

77

SE end which takes you back to the track: one up, two (or three) to go.

Meille na Meine (the mossy peak) is next, one mile down the track on the left, and can be ascended almost anywhere along its entire length. However, it is I think, more enjoyable to traverse its entire ridge, so keep on the track, through the Gharbh Choire ('garve-hhorry', the rough corrie) to 887685. At this point, the unnamed rocky pinnacle ahead, at 887681 (Meall Lochan na Geala on the 1:25,000 scale O.S. sheet - the lochan is on its far side) - challenges by its cheeky appearance. Go first to its summit (good views of Baosbheinn and Beinn an Eoin) starting north again, after a small descent, to do the length of the summit ridge of Meall na Meine from there.

A grassy couloir NNE of the 422m summit takes you to a good vantage point for crossing the marshy ground to ascend the final peak, *Meall Lochan a' Chleirich*. There is an easy approach up a grassy couloir, immediately beyond Lochan a' Chleirich, (877711) to the summit. This little mountain is riddled with rocky buttresses and you may decide to return by the route of your ascent or avoid the worst of them by proceeding down the easier slopes due north to the plantation, but it is possible to find your way down through these buttresses directly NW to the road; but read your O.S. map very carefully in order to locate the long grassy gully which will take you down, and even this gully requires the careful negotiation of minor buttresses and some bum-sliding. This direct descent to the road should not be attempted in mist.

If you are feeling tired after your climb up the Meall a' Ghlas Leothaid and Meall na Meine, give this final peak a miss altogether. The options are open all day on this wild but safe expedition and purists will probably want to take in the little Meall nam Bacan as well. Have a thermos of hot tea and cake in the car, awaiting your return.

Loch na h-Oidhche at the far end of the Flowerdale path.

W11: Through Walks

The Torridon region affords the opportunity for a number of excellent through walks, mostly on good paths or tracks ranging from 8-12 miles, but these will appeal principally to those on camping treks and youth-hostelers who are not faced with the problem of car transport at either end of the walk. For this reason I simply recommend the best of these without going into details. All these walks can, of course, be enjoyed in either direction. The map references are for O.S. sheets 1:50,000 Nos. 19, 24 and 25.

*These walks involving some pathless free-ranging should be avoided during the stalking season.

North Torridon

1.* Glen Grudie (964678) to Glen Torridon (960570), taking in the Coire Mhic Fhearchair (2 miles without path). 9 miles 14.5 km.
2.* Flowerdale (Am Feur Loch, 857721) to Glen Torridon (960570) (via Loch na-h-Oidhche, Lochan Carn na Feola and Loch nan Cabar (3 miles without path). 12 miles 19.3km.
3. Diabaig (790606) to Red Point (731690) via Criag Youth Hostel. Parts of this path are unpleasantly marshy. 7 miles 11.3km.

South Torridon

1. Achnashellach (004484) to Glen Torridon (004581) via Coulin Pass, Loch Coulin and Loch Clair. 8 miles 13km.
2. Achnashellach (004484) to Annat in Glen Torridon (894544) via Coire Lair, Bealach between Sgorr Ruadh and Beinn Liath Mhor, Bealach Ban, Bealach na Lice and Loch an Eion. 11 miles 17.7km.
3. Coulags (958452) to Annat in Glen Torridon (894544) via Fionn Abhainn valley; and thence either (i) via the Bealach between Meall na Ceapairean and Moal Chean Dearg, or (ii) via Loch Coire Fionnaraich and the Bealach na Lice to the Loch an Eion. Thence to Annat. 10-11 miles 16-17.7km
4. Ceann Loch Damh (850476) to Annat in Glen Torridon (894544) via Srath a'Bhathaich and between Beinn Damh and Beinn na h-Eaglaise via the Drochaid Coire Roill. 8 miles 13km.

MOUNTAIN ASCENTS OVER 2,000 FEET

Most hill workers know of Sir Hugh Munro's classification of Scottish peaks over 3,000 feet, known as 'Munros'. There are 284 (2003) of them. A Munro is separate distinctive mountain over 3,000 feet which may also have subsidiary 'tops' over that height. However certain mountains (e.g. Liathach and An Teallach) have more than one summit designated a Munro, which is confusing. Liathach has two Munros, the Spidean a'Choire Leith at 3,456 feet and the Mullach an Rathain at 3,358 feet, as well as other 3,000 feet 'tops'. In the Torridon regions (as defined in this book on p.2) there are nine Munros:- 1. Spidean a'Choire Leith (Liathach); 2. Mullach an Rathain (Liathach); 3. Ruadh-stac Mor, (Beinn Eighe); 4. Spidean Coire nan Clach; 5. Sgurr Mhor; 6. Tom na Gruachaich; 7. Sgorr Ruadh; 8. Maol Chean Dearg; 9. Beinn Liath Mhor and 15 additional 'tops' over 3,000 feet. Slioch, adjacent but outside the region, is also a Munro.

More modest is the Corbett classification, of peaks over 2,500 feet. But the Torridon region has 31 named mountains over 2,000 feet, and since most of these are worthy of attention, the ensuing section deals with the ascent of these.

A number of the Torridon mountains are very steep on all sides (for example Beinn Dearg) yet, in most cases, there is at least one sneaky way up for timid hill walkers like myself where the contours are fairly easy. Some of the summits, on the other hand, can be reached easily by differing routes and in choosing one only for each mountain, I have tried to find the best compromise between distance, ease of ascent and pleasantness of route.

I have arbitrarily grouped these mountains as Northern and Southern to bring some order into the confusion of names, but within each group I have resisted the obvious temptation to list them simply by descending height or even by geographical sub-group, preferring *the order in which I suggest visitors new to the region might most enjoy climbing them.* Beinn an Eoin (of the northern group) is a fine mountain but involves a long slog to get to its main summit and therefore scores low marks but, in due course, is well worth a visit. So Beinn Alligin and Beinn Damh, being easily accessible and very fine mountains, top the lists.

Our two giants, Liathach and Beinn Eighe I have placed at the top of the following list as they must be. I will therefore deal with them

MOUNTAIN ASCENTS OVER 2,000ft

A	NORTHERN GROUP (Numbered N1-N9)	Height		To main summit and back		Page
		m	ft.	Miles	Hours	
1	Liathach	1,054	3,456	3	7	84
2	Beinn Eighe	1,010	3,309	11	7	88
N1	Beinn Alligin	985	3,232	7½	6	91
N2	An Ruadh Mheallan ..	672	2,204	4	3½	96
N3	Beinn Bhreac	624	2,046	11	6	96
N4	Slioch	980	3,217	11	8	98
N5	Beinn a' Chearcaill ..	725	2,380	8	7	101
N6	Beinn an Eoin	855	2,804	14	7½	103
N7	Beinn Dearg	914	2,995	10	8	107
N8	Baosbheinn	875	2,868	12	6	115
N9	Meall a' Ghuibhais ...	878	2,879	(out of bounds)		116
	(mountain trail)	(550)	(1,800)	(2½)	(4)	116

B	SOUTHERN GROUP (Numbered S1–S21)	Height		To main summit and back		Page
		m	ft.	Miles	Hours	
S1	Beinn Damh	902	2,960	7	6½	117
S2	Beinn Liath Mhor	925	3,034	8½	7	122
S3	Sgorr nan Lochane Uaine	860	2,820	7	7	123
S4	Beinn Liath Bheag	800	2,584	9	8	123
S5	Sgurr Dubh	782	2,564	6	5	125
S6	Beinn na h-Eaglaise	737	2,417	7	6	127
S7	(Beinn Shieldaig)	(516)	(1,693)	5	5	129
S8	Beinn Bhan	896	2,969	5½	4	134
S9	Sgurr a' Gharaidh	720	2,361	5	4½	137
S10	Glas Bheinn	711	2332	8½	6½	137
S11	Sgorr Ruadh	960	3,142	7	7	140
S12	Fuar Tholl	907	2,974	9(5)	7½(6)	140
S13	Maol Chean Dearg	933	3,060	12	8	146
S14	Meall nan Ceapairean	670	2,198	11	7	146
S15	Meall Dearg	650	2,132	10	5	149
S16	Beinn a' Chlachain	626	2,053	6	4	150
S17	An Ruadh Stac	892	2,925	7	5½	154
S18	Sgurr a' Ghaoiachain	792	2,600	2*	2*	157
S19	Meall Gorm	710	2,328	1*	1½*	157
S20	Carn Breac	678	2,224	7½	4½	160
S21	Beinn na Feusage	620	2,033			

(* - your car does the work)

The summit of Beinn Eighe, Ruadh Stac Mor (right), from the summit of Liathach. The cone shaped peak to the left is Sail Mhor and between it and Ruadh Stac Mor, beyond and below the ridge joining them, lies the Coire Mhic Fhearchair.

first but they are very special cases, as I shall explain, and not the first mountains to tackle if your experience is limited.

Designated Munros (over 3,000 feet or 914.4 metres) (2003)			
1.	Liathach	- Spidean a Choire Liath	3,456
2.		- Mullach an Rathain	3,358
3.	Beinn Eighe	- Ruadh Stac Mor	3,309
4.		- Spidean Coire nan Clach	3,188
5.	Beinn Alligin	- Sgurr Mhor	3,232
6.		- Tom na Gruagaich	3,024
7.	Sgurr Ruadh		3,142
8.	Beinn Liath Mhor		3,034
9.	Maol Chean Dearg		3,060

LIATHACH AND BEINN EIGHE

If you compare, on relevant maps, the area covered by these two giants with that of the Black Cuillin on Skye, you may be surprised to find that it is the same. The Black Cuillin ridge is a formidable undertaking (except of course for fell tigers) and so are the ridges of Liathach and Beinn Eighe. Anyone considering tackling these two monsters seriously should have no need of this book. However, four main peaks of these two giants can safely be reached, in turn, by ordinary hill walkers with a bit of effort. I will describe these routes before describing the pleasures of the remaining 29 two thousand footers.

1: Liathach ('Leahuhh', the grey one)

Spidean a' Choire Leith 1,054m. 3,456ft. 7 hours.
Mullach an Rathain 1,023m. 3,358ft. 5½ hours.
O.S. sheet 25. (Sheet 24 also for the Mullach.) (Map p.85)

Liathach from the Torridon road.
The only way for the modest hill walker to reach its summit (S)
(Spidean a' Choire Leith) is via the high corrie (arrow).

The main peak of Liathach, the Spidean a' Choire Leith ('speedjan-a-hhorrie-lay', the big peak of the grey corrie) is 3,456ft. above sea level where you start. The relative shortness, in distance, of this ascent is cancelled out by its height and the relentless roughness and steepness of the route which is, however, a safe one with little exposure. The

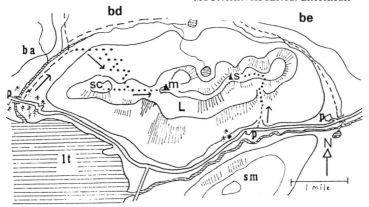

Liathach (L). Routes to the Spidean a' Choire Leith (s), Mullach an Rathain (m) and Sgorr a' Chadail (sc) (....). All other routes, and the pinnacles between the Spidean and the Mullach require considerable experience in mountaineering. Beinn Alligin (ba), Beinn Dearg (bd), Bainn Eighe (be) and Seana Mheallen (sm). Parking places (P). Liathach is a mountain to be reckoned with.

unfit will find it taxing but it is an invigorating experience to visit this summit, the highest in the region.

Park your car in Glen Torridon in the small parking area half a mile beyond the white house in the pine trees (the old Youth Hostel, Glen Cottage) on the Torridon-Kinlochewe road at 931564. Walk 130 paces east down the road to the cairn on the left side of the road which marks the commencement of the path to the summit. It starts across marshy ground and crosses a burn descending from the mountain which, as it cascades down a beautiful gorge, will always be on your left as you ascend to the grey corrie at 1,000 feet. From now on it is rough hard work all the way. As you ascend to the corrie there are a few rocky outcrops to negotiate or by-pass as you prefer.

The corrie is a sloping one and still you have the burn on your left as you ascend the very rough, at first easy, but later steep path beside scree until you reach a sandy (muddy when wet) traverse path heading diagonally up to your right (E). This path ascends by zig-zags up steep but safe heather and grass slopes to the ridge on the skyline. There is one slightly awkward eroded rock-band to negotiate, or scramble past to the right, which the agile will hardly notice. Thereafter the going becomes progressively easier as the path finds its way through rows of small rock buttresses to the ridge. There are no serious problems, but

85

do not attempt this ascent in snow and ice unless you have adequate experience.

The path brings you onto the ridge between the Stuc a' Choire Duibh Bhig (the peak of the little black corrie) to the east and the Bidean Toll a' Mhuic to the west. Ahead are three sizeable bumps to ascend, the Bidean, an unnamed lesser peak and finally the Spidean itself. Each is joined to its neighbour by a narrower ridge, but these 'waists' are wide enough to cause no anxiety, with excellent level paths crossing them.

The approach ridge to the Bidean Toll a' Mhuic is the only narrow crest and one is forced onto a traverse path either to the left (SW) or right (NE). The *right-hand path* is much to be preferred (except in winter and early spring when, due to its location on the north side of the mountain, it may be snowed and iced up). Care is required as you cross this thirty yard path but there is little real sense of exposure. The path is level, firm and steadying handholds are available. Crossing it can be a pleasure. The path to the left (SW side) is in poorer condition and considerably more exposed.

Both paths join to lead to the foot of the Bidean which is your steepest ascent, but the slope is very broad and littered by large quartzite boulders. It is easier to traverse, among large boulders, to the south of the summit of the intermediate peak. The path from now on is indistinct in some places due to the rubble of rocks but the slopes are easy and safe.

As you approach the descent from this middle peak things begin to look a bit formidable. Avoid the path leading down to the right and keep to the crest more to the left. This leads you safely down to a modest slide down a little rock gully (easily re-ascended) onto a broad platform and the path leading gently up to the Spidean, on a wide ridge which becomes rougher and steeper near the summit cairn.

The views from the top are glorious, especially of the pinnacle ridge ahead and of the Coire na Caime (the crooked corrie) to the north below the pinnacles, and back down the ridge that you have ascended and along the adjacent Beinn Eighe ridge to the east. Descend again by the route that you came, taking in Liathach's most easterly peak the Stuc a' Choire Duibh Bhig (3,000ft) if you feel so inclined. Those over sixty may feel free to use the occasional 'six point' contact (two feet, two hands and the two cheeks of your bottom) at moments during the descent.

The *Mullach an Rathain* ('mullahh-an r'han', the hill of the pulley). This peak lies at the western end of the pinnacle ridge and the Coire

View from the summit of Liathach, looking east to Beinn Eighe, draped in white quartzite scree.

na Caime and be warned that this exercise requires experience and fortitude. An experienced girl climber fell into Coire na Caime to her death from here in 1985. Do not be fooled either by those who tell you that an 'easy' path traverses on the left so that you can by-pass the pinnacles. It is insubstantial and leaves you very exposed in places.

The safe, easy, but long way to the summit of Mullach an Rathain is up behind the mountain via the Coire Mhic Nobuil, but when you reach the top the views are as magnificent as from the Spidean and you will have again Munro'd. Leave your car at the Beinn Alligin car park (O.S. sheet 24, 869576) and ascend NE up the excellent path of the Coire Mhic Nobuil. At 882589 do *not* cross the river by the bridge but leave the path and begin to traverse, ascend and zig-zag up the rough slopes which lead to the huge broad ridge between Sgorr a' Chadail and the Mullach an Rathain. Once you have gained the ridge, note the spot, pending your descent, and consider first visiting this most westerly of Liathach's peaks (2,297ft.) before turning back for the 1½ mile moorland walk to the summit of the Mullach; very easy going, with a final curved little ridge of 30 yards or so to the very top, but be warned that these final slopes, if glaciated in winter, could precipitate you into the village below if you slipped. There is no 'exposure' or difficulty anywhere on this ascent in summer conditions with good visibility, but I admit that it is somewhat of a slog.

2: Beinn Eighe

Ruadh-stac Mor 1,010m. 3,309ft. 7 hours.
Spidean Coire nan Clach 972m. 3,188ft. 5 hours.
O.S. sheets 19 and 25. (Map p.89)

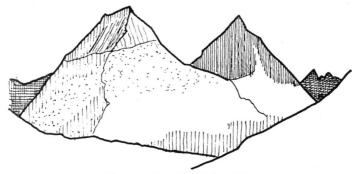

The summit peak of Beinn Eighe.
Ruadh-stac Mor (left), and Sail Mhor (right), from Glen Grudie.
The Coire Mhic Fhearchair lies between them.

Beinn Eighe (Ben-'A', the 'ice mountain', if you are a romantic, or 'the comb mountain' after its serrated toothy ridge if you are more matter-of-fact), stands next to Liathach and together they form a huge mountain complex, with only the valley of the Coire Dubh Mor separating them, some 10 miles long. But these two mountains could hardly be more different, Liathach gaunt, grey and forbidding, Beinn Eighe graceful and inviting in its long drapes of white quartzite scree and elegant peaks shaped like cones. Two of Beinn Eighe's peaks are accessible to timid but strong-willed hill walkers.

Ruadh-stac Mor (3,309ft.) 7 hours.
This is Beinn Eighe's highest summit and is most easily reached *via the Coire Mhic Fhearchair (see Walk No.1).* There are no alarms but it is a long way and the 800ft slog up steep scree, rocks and grass at the end of the Coire requires either a bold heart or an insensitive degree of youth and fitness. (See p.51)

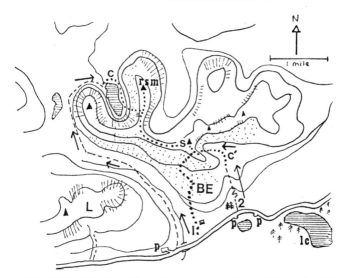

Beinn Eighe (BE). Feasible route to two summits for the modest hill walker (....)   1. To the main summit Ruadh-stac Mor (rsm) (3,309ft) via the Coire Mhic Fhearchair (C)   2. To the Spidean Coire nan Clach (S) (3,188ft) via the Coire an Laoigh (C'). Loch Clair (lc).
Parking places (p). Both ascents end with a scramble up steep scree.
Treat this mountain with respect.

Spidean Coire nan Clach (the peak of the stony corrie), 3,188ft. 5 hours.
hours.
This is a short ascent. Find a spot to ease your car into near the beginning of the delightful stalker's path which will lead you up to the fabulous Coire an Laoigh ('corrie-an-lowie', the corrie of the calf: and your own calves may consider this well named). The tiny plantation of pine trees marks the beginning (977578). The inviting place to leave your car has for years been blocked by boulders, presumably for conservation reasons, but two cars can squeeze into its entrance if one hog hasn't taken up the whole space by parking centrally in the limited space. These boulders have recently been pushed aside but may be put back. There is a similar place 200 yards farther along the road (E) round the bend. (The official Torridon car park is 1½ miles to the west of this spot.) After 100 yards of marsh this path becomes a delight all the way to the corrie, where it peters out. The corrie itself is also a delight; aim straight ahead. The grass and scree slopes facing

89

you are not a delight, they are annoyingly steep; steeper than they look as you approach. (See note below.) Keep to the left-hand side on grass where a zig-zagging path will do its best for you. The rocks dead centre are wet, slippery and therefore dangerous, and the scree above them and to the right really miserable unless you are a scree-cat. Once you have gained the shoulder there is a stony but broad ridge to the top and the view of Liathach westward is extremely fine. Experienced ridge walkers may consider proceeding west along the ridge from Spidean Coire nan Clach towards Ruadh-stac Mor in order to descend and return by the Coire Mhic Fhearchair.

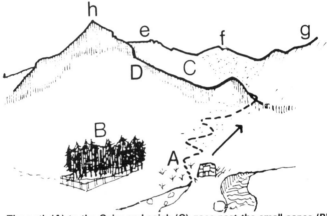

The path (A) to the Coire an Laoigh (C) goes past the small copse (B).
Spidean Coire nan Clach (e), Sgurr nan Fhir Duibhe (f), Sgurr Ban (g) and
the Stuc Coire an Laoigh (h). An approach to the main ridge via the
shoulder of the Stuc (D) is not recommended.

NOTE

There is an alternative approach to the Spidean via the Coire nan Clach (965596) which lies below this summit, but it has none of the pleasures of the stalkers' path to the Coire an Laoigh nor the frisson of the scramble up the steep slopes at the latter's western end. It is a somewhat relentless and pathless 2,000ft. slog up moderately steep heather, grass and rock slopes, starting up the track to the ruined dwelling 100 yards beyond (E) the bridge (961570). A path leads on beyond the ruin but becomes indistinct as it heads up the Coire Dubh Mor on the east side of the river gorge. After ½ mile leave it and head NNE up marshy and rough terrain aiming well to the left (W) of the low humpy rock buttresses ahead. Once above these, veer to the right

(NE) up rocky and grassy ground to reach the shallow sloping floor of the Coire nan Clach at 964593 and thence directly ahead up easy slopes to gain the ridge (col) between the Spidean and the Stuc Coire an Laoigh, at 966595.

You might, however, consider this as a route of descent, if you did not enjoy the steep climb out of the Coire an Laoigh on your way up. If so, descend from the col and make for the far left-hand bottom corner of the Coire nan Clach (WSW). Thence continue WSW (compass bearing 225°) until you are beyond the rock buttresses, at first invisible below you to your left. Then descend SSW down heather and grass slopes and then S over flatter marshy ground to the ruin at 961570 and the road.

NORTHERN GROUP

N1: Beinn Alligin 985m 3,232ft.

O.S sheet 24.   Total distance and time:
Tom na Graugaich, 3,024ft. - 5 miles 8km. 5 hours;
Sgurr Mhor, 3,323ft. - 7 ¹/₂ miles 12km, 6 hours;
Complete traverse - 8 miles 13km, 7-8 hours. (Map p.93)

Beinn Alligin in winter from the road to Shieldaig

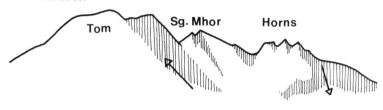

This is fine mountain, which dominates the north shore of Loch Torridon, has three components, Tom na Graugaich (the hill of the fair young person), Sgurr Mhor (big peak) and the Alligin Horns; Sgurr Mhor and Tom na Gruagaich being designated Munros. The hill walker has the choice of ascending one or two of these peaks or of doing the complete traverse, the Horns being comparable, but not similar, to Helvellyn's Striding Edge. Poucher recommends doing the circuit in an anticlockwise direction, Horns first. I advise the opposite, clockwise, direction, doing Tom na Gruagaich first. If you attempt the Horns first and do not like them you can only retreat with a sense of failure. The other way the Tom is a fine climb, Sgurr Mhor ('sgurr-vor) even better and the Horns can then be studied from the top of the main summit and a decision made. If you decide on retreat at this stage, you have climbed two Munros and you need not return by the way came if you still want to see more of the Horns without traversing their airy up and down narrow summit ridges.

Leave your car at the Beinn Alligin car park (869576). A path leads diagonally off north under a silver birch opposite the park; it leads through marshy and muddy escarpments to the bowl which is the key to your ascent of the Tom. In earlier times there was a wooden bridge over the river, about half a mile up the track up Coire Mhic Nobuil, which facilitated a more direct uphill approach to Bein Alligin's 'bowl' (the key to the summit). But as this was causing severe scarring of the marshy ground the NTS demolished the bridge, which may never be replaced. The present recommended route commencing opposite the car park is also scarred, but I suppose that one wound to the mountain's flank is better than two!

As you enter the bowl (or corrie) the path picks up again and you now ascend this magnificent stony corrie. As you near the top of the bowl the tendency is to be drawn on half-left where the path peters out, whereas the summit is more to the right (NNE), but it does not

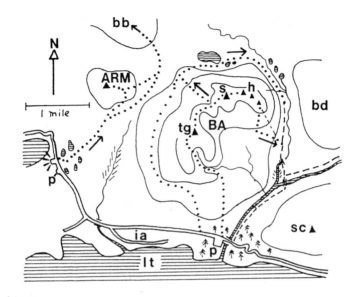

Recommended routes for Beinn Alligin (BA), An Ruadh Mheallan (ARM)
and Beinn Bhreac (bb)....Alternatives are shown as....
Sgorr a' Chadail (sc), Beinn Dearg (bd), Inveralligin (ia), Loch Torridon (lt)
For Beinn Alligin leave your car at the Alligin car park (p):
Tom na Gruagaich (tg), Sgurr Mhor (s), Horns of Alligin (h).
For An Ruadh Mheallan leave your car off the road at (p). The walk can be
extended to Beinn Bhreac if you fancy a long day over rough ground.

matter as you come onto a broad flat plateau either way when the
gently rising summit cone declares itself. The ascent of the snowfield,
which lingers on this corrie and can become glaciated can be
dangerous.

It is also a simple matter to get yourself down all the way from Sgurr
Mhor if you happen to get misted out while up there, as you simply
follow the obvious easy ridge south-west and south as far as the
cairned summit of the Tom. The only place that needs a careful
compass bearing is from the summit of the Tom to the top of the bowl.

Hill walkers crossing the ridge from Tom na Gruagaich to Sgurr Mhor (Beinn Alligin).

One has to descend again more to the *right* than one tends to imagine, so obey your compass. Once in the bowl it can only deliver you safely, if roughly, onto the lower slopes and thence back to the path or the road, but low cloud and mist are below the bowl anyway. So, as you stand on the Tom's fine cairned summit, with impressive views not only of Sgurr Mhor's plunging precipices but beyond them north as far as An Teallach and south-west to the northern aspect of Liathach, it is a good moment to take a retrospective compass bearing to the upper part of the corrie from whence you have just come if the weather seems changeable. If that is 'it' for you, you have achieved two Munro's and can return at leisure the way you came. To others, Sgurr Mhor with is huge cleft will beckon irresistibly.

The ridge (1 mile) from the Tom to Sgurr Mhor is very fine, adequately broad not to cause the slightest anxiety, and easy going. You descend a bit steeply at first from the Tom with sheer precipices to your right, but you are never close enough to them to cause any anxiety. Just before you reach the grassy flat part of the ridge there is one small obstacle. You have to descend a piece of rock face no higher than a door, but smooth. The young do not notice it and couples of any age simply help each other up and down it, but alone you will either have to take a chancy drop of a couple of feet or take to the unpleasantly steep scree to your left (precipices to your right) to get round it. But surmount this little difficulty you must, as the rest of the way to the very fine summit of Sgurr Mhor (and your second Munro) is easy and should not be missed, and you do not have to return this way if you do not wish to. So once down the rock it is worth considering how you plan to get up it again if you are alone (a 'stirrup' leg up for one followed by a hand up for the other solves the problem for two) before making this decision. However you do not have to return this way even if you do not wish to traverse the Horns.

On your way to the summit of Sgurr Mhor an intermediate bump presents. Go over the top for the best views in fine weather, but keep a little below on its north-west side on windy days. It is easy going on a path right to the top now but allow a few minutes to take the diversionary path to the right which leads to the great cleft on the south face of this mountain so you can gaze down its awesome depths. Before you make the final ascent, note that you have 800ft. of grass slopes on your left (WNW) leading to the An-Reidh-choire. This is your alternative way down if you do not fancy the Horns and also prefer not to go back to Tom na Gruagaich. From the summit you have a panoramic view of the Horns. There are three of them, the smallest (and farthest from you) having a sub-pimple making in fact a small fourth Horn.

I am not recommending the traverse of the Horns to the modest hill walker because it involves some fairly easy clambering in somewhat exposed positions, but the scrambling is not hard and the young and experienced will enjoy it. I would say it rates about with Helvellyn's Striding Edge, though different in character. You will have to make an assessment from the summit of Sgurr Mhor or go down the long descent from the Sgurr to have a closer look. You can always retreat and take the easy slopes from the saddle south-west of the summit and then walk *round* the Horns at a low level by the Loch Toll nam Biast (870620).

The ascent of the first Horn and descent from the second are the steepest. The traverse of the first Horn is along the crest of a long ridge but is only dangerous if iced or in high winds. The descent from the second Horn is steep and rough but wide. As you approach the third, smallest, Horn an apparent impasse presents in the form of a 15 foot rock face, but a small path to the right leads quickly to a rock gully and a moderate scramble up it leading to the summit cairn. From there it is easy and safe going along the crest to a sub-pimple and thence to the broad south-east shoulder. It is better to do this than to keep on this traverse path which by-passes this Horn on the south side, as it is poor in quality and crosses steep unstable ground.

After completing the last Horn you descend by steep rough ground to a broad flat shoulder. The path and cairns lead to the extreme east end and a steep very rough and eroded descent down its final slopes: it is easier and more pleasant to go directly SW and SSW down more gentle grass slopes to your right, commencing among boulders, swinging east again to join the path for a final 2½ mile walk to the car park. (Poucher indicates this alternative descent route on Plate 114, Route 46, in his book *The Scottish Peaks* pub: Constable). The other way is for insensitive boots and leathery bottoms.

If you are an inexperienced and timid scrambler, but have an experienced companion, take 30 feet of light climbing rope, a proper waist band and clip (karabiner) so that he or she can help you up and down the awkward bits, and you will enjoy the trip. Young hill walkers experience no difficulties in traversing the Horns.

If you elect not to tackle the Horns your pleasures are by no means over. Descend again to the lowest point of the saddle below (southwest) of Sgurr Mhor and descend north-west down the easy grass slopes to level ground. Now continue your expedition by walking north and then east keeping close to the crags of Sgurr Mhor. Keep south of Loch Toll nam Biast, but north of the two subsequent small lochans, though this doesn't matter much. This and the rest of the walk round the Horns is simply the reverse of that described in *Walk No.2* (walk round Beinn Alligin). Alternatively, but not so good, is to walk south-west and then south round the west side of Tom na Gruagaich also as described in Walk No.2 (p.53).

Don't be put off by the fact that every hill walker visiting the region climbs Beinn Alligin. It is fine mountain, a 'must', gives you one Munro and a 3,000ft. 'top' and is never busy.

N2/3: An Ruadh Mheallan and Beinn Bhreac 672m 2,204ft. and 624m 2,046ft.

O.S sheet 24. Distance 4 or 11 miles. 6.4 or 17.7km. Time 3 ¹/₂ or 6 hours. (Map p.93)

An Ruadh Mheallan ('An-rua-vellen', the red hill), in spite of its relatively small size manages to raise a proud head against its massive neighbour, Beinn Alligin, 1½ miles to the east. The easiest ascent is made from the road at the viewpoint at 824594, but this is only a small

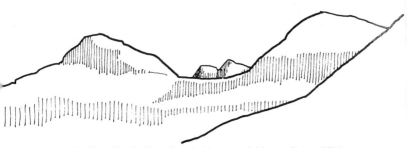

An Ruadh Mheallan (left) is dwarfed by its neighbours Beinn Alligin
(right) and Baosbheinn (middle distance).

parking area for two or three cars and, as people like to come in their
cars to enjoy the view, it is more helpful to leave your car a hundred
yards down the road (towards Alligin Shuas) where a suitable space
can be found opposite the small lochan (see map on p.93). Walk back
up the road to the viewpoint from where a little path ascends from the
east side of the road. This leads over the first crest and then seems to
disappear so, if you fail to find it, this is not very important. Proceed
over marshy and complicated ground directly NE for a mile towards
your little mountain, passing on either side of Loch nan Tri Eileanan.
You then cross a broad valley before ascending the east shoulder of the
mountain up the easiest slopes and thence, a little more steeply, NW,
to the broad summit. The views from the top of Beinn Alligin's west
face are particularly impressive.

From An Ruadh Mheallan it is a 3½ mile slog over rough country to
the summit of Beinn Bhreac ('Ben-vrecki', the speckled mountain) as
one has to take a semi-circular route, going E, NE, N and NW, in
order to avoid losing height unnecessarily which a more direct route
beside Loch Gaineamhach Beag would involve. About the only reason
to tempt one to make this trip over wild terrain is an obsession to
climb all the two thousand footers in the region but, when climbed,
the view of Baosbheinn and retrospective view of the NW flank of
Beinn Alligin are most impressive and rewarding. The summit, a
broad flat bowling green of fine moss littered with flat sandstone slabs
is uncairned. There must be few people who bother to visit it but the
deer will welcome you. A return journey, passing E or W of An Ruadh
Mheallan, avoids re-ascending this peak. Beinn Bhreac lies deep in the
National Trust area and this walk should not be attempted during the
stalking season of September 1-November 21 without special
permission. It would also be unwise to attempt it in misty conditions.

97

**Baosbheinn and Beinn Bhreac (middle distance) from the summit of
An Ruadh Mheallan, in winter.**

N4: **Slioch**   980m   3,217ft.

*O.S sheet 19. Distance 11 miles 17.7km. Time 8 hours. (Map p.99).
This climb should not be undertaken during the estate's shooting season, mid-
August to February*

Those familiar with the view of Slioch as the huge square buttress of
rock dominating Loch Maree, have to walk to Lochan Fada via the
Heights of Kinlochewe to see why this mountain has been named the

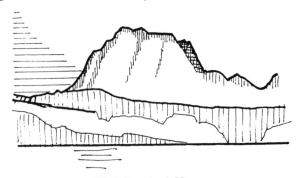

Slioch from Loch Maree.

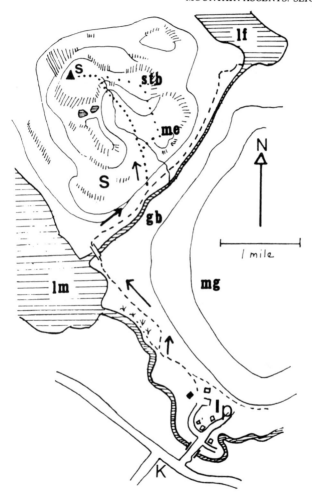

The long walk and ascent of Slioch from Kinlochewe (K) and Incheril
(I). Park your car in the signposted car park at (p). Mheallan Gobhar
(mg), Gleann Bianasdail (gb), Meall Each (me) Sgurr an Tuill Bhain
(stb), summit of Slioch (s). Loch Maree (lm) and Lochan Fada (lf).
Sgurr Dubh (S). Note diversion in path 1 mile from Incheril (see p.70)

'spear'. (Alternatively 'sliabhach', place of slopes.) It is because of the appearance of the Sgurr an Tuill Bhain its westerly subsidiary peak, a sharp pointed slanting cone, which dominates from that side. The ascent of Slioch is a slog, but a rewarding one and beautiful all the way. It is because of its accessibility from Kinlochewe and also because it is a Munro that I have presumed to include it among the Torridon peaks. Although rough going in places, it presents no anxieties or difficulties in fine weather.

Park your car at Incheril and walk to Gleann Bianasdail (see Walk No.7 for details of the first 3 miles). After you have crossed the bridge (013657) follow the path NE across marshy ground and look for a cairn after half a mile marking the commencement of the path which, in due course, ascends on the left-hand side of a burn descending between Sgurr Dubh and Meall Each. This is a rough but easy ascent which leads to the magnificent and huge high Coire na Sleaghaich (corrie of the slog?) - so named on the 1:25,000 O.S. sheet, which is the key to your ascent to the summit. This point of arrival usually calls for some refreshment before proceeding.

You may be able to find the track which leads you up to the saddle between the Slioch summit and Sgurr Dubh (S) past two large lochans and thence via a scramble up onto the huge summit plateau. The less adventurous and very pleasant route is to aim NNW straight across the corrie to the waterfall at its far end (014687) and there pick up a definite path ascending on the left-hand side of the tumbling burn to reach the summit plateau and thence, over excellent ground, WNW to the summit. From here the views in all directions are magnificent, particularly of Slioch's near Fisherfield neighbours, A' Mhaighdean ('a' Vuhhvayn', the maiden) and Mullach Coire Mhic Fhearchair.

You can vary your route of descent by walking over flat stony ground due east to the summit of Sgurr an Tuill Bhain (the peak of the white hollow) and thence down its easy slopes SSE towards Meall Each (the hill of the horse) which delightful little summit is worth the compliment of a visit. *Classic Walks* (Diadem) advises a return journey thence via Gleann Bianasdail, Lochan Fada and the heights of Kinlochewe, but this exciting possibility will add a further 4½ miles on to your expedition but is something you could justifiably boast about in the hotel lounge later that evening (see Walk No.7).

N5: Beinn a' Chearcaill   725m   2,380ft.

O.S. sheet 19.   Distance 8-9 miles 13-14.5km.   Time 7 hours. (Map p.102)

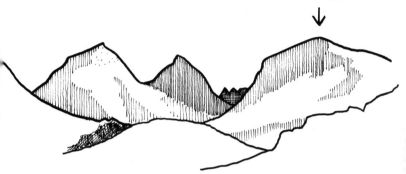

Beinn a' Chearcaill (↓) from Glen Grudie, its thunder stolen by the great peaks of Beinn Eighe (Ruadh-stac Mor and Sail Mhor) and Liathach in the background.

Beinn a' Chearcaill is accessible from the excellent stalker's path in Glen Grudie and constitutes, in effect, a high moorland walk offering a dress-circle view of the great Torridonian backsides (Ruadh-stac Beag, Ruadh-stac Mor, Coire Mhic Fhearchair, Sail Mhor, Liathach, Beinn Dearg, Sgurr Mhor and Beinn an Eoin). It is one of the Flowerdale group and stands between Beinn an Eoin to the west and Meall a' Ghuibhais to the east.

The stalker's path, which traverses Glen Grudie from the southern shores of Loch Maree, commences at the white house at 964678, ¼ mile beyond the Bridge of Grudie as you travel from Kinlochewe towards Gairloch. The house stands among trees, but is easily seen as you approach and there is room to park your car on the firm stony grass adjacent to the roadside 25 yards or so beyond the drive leading to the house. Proceed up the drive, which leads you directly to the path which diagonals across the house's garden, trying not to feel like a guilty trespasser as you go. This excellent track leads you SSW well above the River Grudie which is below on your left. The views of Ruadh-stac Mor and Sail Mhor ahead are impressive. After 1½ miles you reach the edge of the rather solemn Coire Briste. Watch out for the small cairn on the right side of your path at 953657 which indicates a much rougher, smaller, and in places indistinct, path which will lead you upwards and across the northern slopes of this corrie onto the

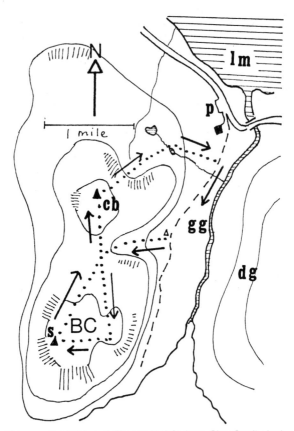

**The ascent of Beinn a' Chearcaill (BC) from Glen Grudie (gg).
Leave your car just beyond the drive to the warden's house and find the
path by going up the drive and past the house. Summit of Beinn a'
Chearcaill (s), a' Choineach Beinn (cb), Druim Grudaidh (dg),
Loch Maree (lm).**

broad saddle between Beinn a' Chearcaill S, and a' Choineach Beag
N. You will reach a burn and lochan and the massive flat top of Beinn
a' Chearcaill lies one mile due south up rough but easy slopes and
rocky outcrops. It is worth making a circular tour of this huge plateau
once you are on it since the walking is excellent and such a route pays

proper tribute to the mountain's name, Beinn a' Chearcaill ('ben-a-cherkell', the circular mountain). But the best reason for doing this is to enjoy to the full the splendid views of the northern aspects of the adjacent Torridonian giants to the east, south and west. Since the real summit lies more remotely to the west of the plateau, I suggest you go clockwise and aim first for the unnamed prominence at 944641 from which the views down into Beinn Eighe's Coire Mhic Fhearchair are dramatic. From there a gentle arc of a circle west across good ground brings you to the fine flat sandstone slabs of the true summit (725m) at 932638, from which the panoramic views of Beinn Dearg and Beinn an Eoin are the principal features.

There is no need to retrace your steps for the descent as you can have a bit of fun finding your way more directly down the rocky slopes from the summit and between lochans going NNE back to the flat saddle area above Coire Briste. From there you can return, via this corrie, to the Glen Grudie path, but it makes a better day of it to return by climbing, due north, to the three little summits of a' Choineach Beag (the little moss). From the most northerly and highest summit, proceed and descend in a NE direction to find and descend by a rough but delightful valley between cliffs which commences at 943666. This will lead you toward the largish Loch a' Choin Bhain 1 mile away to the NNE. However, in order to avoid the cliffs to the north between the loch and the road it is best to veer to your right ENE to the little unnamed lochan at 951671, from the far E side of which there is an easy descent down the slopes beside, or away from, the burn, descending ESE back to the Glen Grudie path, joining it at or about 958668. An excellent expedition for a fine day, it is best avoided when there is low cloud or mist as the terrain is an extensive rough and complicated wilderness.

N6: Beinn an Eoin 855m 2,804ft.

O.S sheet 19.   14 miles 22.5km. 7 ¹/₂ hours.   (Map.105)

Beinn an Eoin's summit is the farthest away from roads and civilisation of all the Torridon peaks, yet approached up the track to Loch na h-Oidhche, and along its 1½ mile long and lovely ridge, its ascent offers an excellent day with little sense of having done a wearisome plod to achieve it. The summit is nearest to the road at the Loch Maree Hotel, but three miles of rough wet terrain lies between you and the mountain and this route culminates (if you can find it) in a

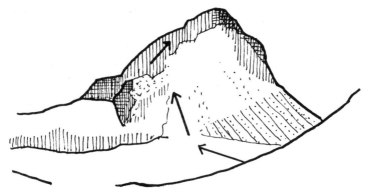

The northern end of Beinn an Eoin and the suggested route of initial ascent to reach its long north-south ridge leading to the summit.

path which zig-zags up a very steep grass slope near the summit, missing out a mile of delightful ridge walking. I therefore advise an approach via the Loch na h-Oidhche track even though you actually have to walk 1½ miles further in each direction. But what could be more pleasant?

Park your car by the corrugated iron barn opposite Am Feur Loch, on the Kinlochewe to Gairloch road, at 857721. Proceed south along the track through increasingly wild country for 3½ miles. At first only gloomy Boasbheinn is visible far away to your right, Beinn an Eoin being hidden behind Meille na Meine (the mossy peak). When your mountain does come into view you are only seeing its most *northenly* butttress although you may have glimpsed its elongated ridge and higher summit from the road as you approached Loch Maree Hotel, if you came in that direction.

Cross the stepping stones at 886676 (if wet and slippery cross 15 yards upstream) and then proceed directly SE over somewhat wet and rough terrain for ⅓ mile to reach and ascend a rocky and grassy gully which commences at 894674. A tiny waterfall tumbles into the top end of this gully feeding a small, at times subterranean, burn which will be your companion as you ascend. (If staying in the gully does not please you, use the steepish but easy rock and grass slopes on your left.) A slightly steeper exit from the gully leads to a huge tilted sandstone platform, and upon a further one stands a handsome cairn which will be a useful marker for your return journey. This and many other sandstone slabs in the vicinity reassure one that this is a sandstone and grass, and not a quartzite, mountain. Praise be! Proceeding at first

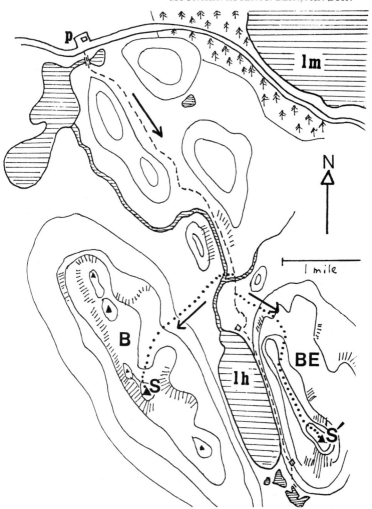

The long walks to the summits of Beinn an Eoin (s') and Baosbheinn (s).
Park your car by the barn at Am Feur Loch (p). The three mile walk
towards Loch na h-Oidhche (lh) is, however, along an excellent path. It
is when you have to leave it that the rough stuff begins.
Loch Maree (lm).

obliquely south and to your right easy grass terraces lead west directly to Beinn an Eoin's ridge, as near to the most northerly end as you choose. A mile of beautiful ridge walking in a SE direction follows. The ridge is very broad, with a few small ups and downs, with fine moss and sandstone slabs underfoot. As you approach, after a mile, a sudden, apparently steep, ascent ahead you may notice the Talladale 'path' zig-zagging up very steep grass slopes to your left (east). You will also notice that the ridge you are traversing is beginning to narrow and the ascent ahead looks as though it could be a bit nasty. It isn't, its threat is just a bluff. The slope (starting at 901652) is not steep and is very wide and you are well away from the plunging precipices to your left and the steep scree slopes over on your right. Go straight up. In due course you will become acquainted with a somewhat crazy and eroded apology for a zig-zag path, made presumably by boots, but which offers no advantage (rather the reverse) to continuing your direct ascent up grass and sandstone slabs.

On surmounting this non-obstacle (an easy 200ft. ascent) you will find yourself on a delightful mossy and grassy plateau whence proceed SSE towards the summit cairn. As you advance confidently and joyfully towards it, you will find your grassy ridge narrowing gradually, down to about 4 feet in width. Steep slopes are on each side and minor sandstone obstacles appear just when you wish that they wouldn't. One of these demands a small descent and then a squeeze, past a trifling sandstone buttress, to the left, on a little bit of path which shows you what to do. On such occasions, one must concentrate on the job in hand and ignore what is (or rather what is not) on either side of you. The summit plateau is quite close (50 yards) and you are already almost at the same level when you commence your traverse of this narrow bit of ridge. The sight of the cairn will surely suck you on.

Beinn an Eoin is, geographically, a simple shape. On my first ascent, cloud and rain, which had been following me all the way up the ridge, overtook me as I reached the cairn. Fairly thick cloud then persisted for the rest of the day down to 1,000ft., but I had no difficulty in finding my way back to the cairn at the head of the original gully of ascent using four sequential compass bearings. I mention this to remind you again that when walking on these hills one should always have in mind how one is going to get down in the event of a mist out.

Beinn an Eoin means the mountain of the bird, but it is also the haunt of deer. Verdict: highly recommended.

N7: **Beinn Dearg** 914m 2,995ft.

O.S sheets 19/25. Distance 10 miles 16km. Time 8 hours.
(Long route to summit.) (Map p.109)

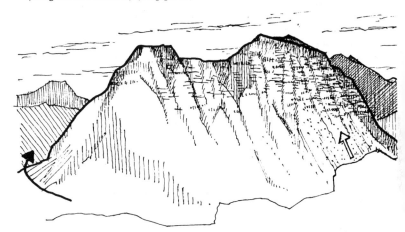

The SW face of Beinn Dearg as seen from the Horns of Beinn Alligin.
Beinn Dearg's summit is guarded by relentlessly steep slopes riddled
with rocky buttresses and narrow approach ridges. The commonly
recommended route to the summit, suitable for the energetic and
fearless, is up the very steep slopes and between the buttresses near
the SW corner (white arrow). The only route which avoids all such
hazards is round the N side of the mountain (black arrow).

Beinn Dearg ('Ben jerrag', the red hill) is a great mountain the top of
whose summit cairn reaches above 3,000 feet, but unless one is
prepared to face severe steepness and/or approach ridges with
exposure ranging from moderate to severe, there is only one totally
scare-free way to reach it. This is at the expense of a very long trek
over rough country to the north side to ascend the steep slopes below
the summit above the Loch a' Choire Mhoir (899609). Irvine Butterfield in *The High Mountains, a Guide for Mountain Walkers* warns of its
difficulties giving his opinion that it is a mountain 'unsuitable for
inexperienced parties in bad weather', and it might therefore seem
best for me simply to say that this is a mountain that should be left to
experienced scramblers and deter more modest hill walkers. This I
cannot do for my various excursions around and upon it have caused

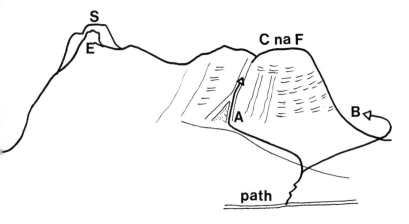

**Recommended direct ascent of the SE face of Carn na Feola (A).
Longer route, but easier ascent, from the north (B). Summit of Beinn
Dearg (S), the 'Enemy' (E).**

me to come to love it in spite of its appearance of unrelenting ferocity.
There are various real pleasures still to be had, from simply climbing
its most easterly and accessible peak, the Carn na Feola, to visiting
and assessing at first hand the main summit approach ridges.

Before describing the long way round from the north I will offer
some comments on the more usually recommended routes, for only
cowards like myself, scared of exposure but filled with an obstinate
desire to reach the top, rather than face again the steep and dangerous
western cliffs or the 'enemy' on the eastern approach ridge, would
dream of walking all the way round to the back (north) side of the
mountain in order to get up it.

To the west, south and east Beinn Dearg presents an unbroken wall
of very steep slopes and precipices which confront the walker uninvit-
ingly as he or she approaches up the Coire Mhic Nobuil path.
However, the route of ascent usually recommended is up the steep SW
flank below the summit. Three streams descend from high up the
mountain at this point (888604). Grass and scree slopes between these
lead through serrated rows of rock precipices which can be turned as
one struggles fearfully upwards. If you manage to negotiate these and
have the will to reach the narrow and somewhat complicated crest of
the ridge it will then lead you directly to the summit but it requires
some clambering and some nerve to do this. However, a descent by

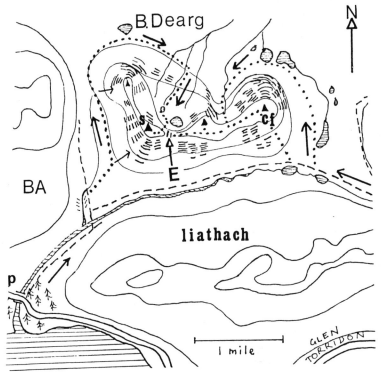

The approach to the summit of Beinn Dearg (s): from the east via the Coire Dubh Mor and Carn na Feola (cf) is blocked by 'the enemy' (E) for those unable to cope with an extremely exposed traverse. The approach from the west, via the Coire Mhic Nobuil, involves a long rough walk round to the north side for hill walkers unwilling to tackle the steep buttressed slopes on the west side immediately below the summit (s). Car park at (p).

these same slopes is far more hazardous because of the rows of rock cliffs which are far easier to see and thus to avoid as you go up than when you attempt to come down from above them. So, if you do decide to take this, the shortest way to the summit, note and mark carefully your path of ascent and attempt to return precisely by the same route. Another favoured route from this side is to climb the slightly less steep slopes at the NW end of Stuc na Cabhaig in order to

109

enjoy the, at times narrow and exposed, ridge walk south to the main summit. I cannot, however, recommend either of these routes unless you are already an experienced scrambler with a head for heights.

Carn na Feola and the eastern approach

Carn na Feola (the peak of the flesh), Beinn Dearg's most easterly summit, is well worth climbing in its own right as it affords the very best views of the northern aspect of Liathach and its famous pinnacle ridge the Am Fasarinen, albeit with the sun behind them in the middle of the day. It will also give you the opportunity of visiting the 'enemy', a great castle of rock which defends the main summit from this side, as well as climbing the unnamed intermediate summit at 906608. If you feel able to traverse the 'enemy' you can reach the main summit this way. If not you can return to the summit of Carn na Feola on your way back.

Leave your car at the Glen Torridon car park and take the path up the Coire Dubh Mor, which goes behind the NE side of Liathach (see Walk No.1 - 'Coire Mhic Fhearchair'). Continue up this path for 3 miles passing the cairns on your right indicating the subsidiary track leading to the Coire Mhic Fhearchair after 2½ miles. As you approach Beinn Dearg you will see its long bulky ridge leading to the main summit at the farther (west) end, and below it the 'enemy' is distinctly visible in clear weather. You will also begin to see the long grassy slope at the east end of the south face which is the route I recommend for the direct ascent of Carn na Feola (see p.108). The path now begins to deteriorate and becomes marshy and muddy in places. When you are about opposite the Loch nan Cabar (925605), which is not visible and ½ mile to the north, strike due north across lumpy moraine ground towards the western side of this loch. You will now be opposite the SE corner of Carn na Feola and will have to decide whether to ascend directly up the steep slopes which face you (these unfortunately become steeper as you get higher), negotiating the rock buttresses as you go, or to walk right round the great mass of Carn na Feola in order to reach the Coire Beag (the little corrie) on the north side where the slopes leading to the summit ridge are easy.

You must make your own decision here, but I can advise that the direct approach is considerably easier and less hazardous than the SW approach up the western slopes to the main summit which I have already described. Three grassy slopes can be seen ascending the extreme east end of Beinn Dearg's south face. The farthest and longest of these, looking like an inverted fork, is entirely free of rock buttresses and offers a safe hands and feet clamber to the top. This

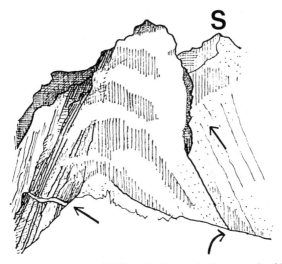

The 'enemy' barring the trepid hill walker's way to the summit of Beinn Dearg from the east. The very steep, but relatively safe, screes to the right (→) offer a less alarming alternative to the exposed wretched little path on the left (←), but involve the loss of 400 feet in height and the subsequent long climb back up the steep but safe slopes below the summit (S).

long grassy couloir also offers a safe bottom-sliding descent but would be difficult to locate from the top if you have ascended from the north side via the Coire Beag.

If you decide to take the very long but easy way up round the back, aim to make a wide sweep in the arc of a circle, going close by the western shores of Lochan Carn na Feola, in order to avoid the worst of the vast array of huge boulders strewn across the ground to the N and NNE corner of this peak. The extra distance will actually save you time and frustration. Crossing this wilderness area is mostly good under foot and deer, unused to visitors, abound. Once you reach the mouth of the little corrie itself, all is plain sailing. The slopes at the head of the corrie look a trifle off-putting as you approach them, but as is so often the case in head-on approaches, their threat is a sham and, to one's pleasure, it is an ascent beside a small stream, up easy grass slopes to the saddle and the fine views of Liathach's pinnacle ridge. Reserve the ascent to the summit Carn na Feola for your return. First you must exercise your powers of discretion at 900607. Move due

111

west over sloping and ascending ground and gradually the 'enemy' will come into view. The broad sloping ridge above the Loch a' Choire Mhoir narrows abruptly to about nine feet and standing right across it is a huge and challenging 'gendarme'.

This fairly sorts out the 'men and women' from the 'boys and girls' and I am definitely of the latter group. To the right cliffs and steep scree plunge down to the Lochan a' Choire Mhoir. To the left rocky precipices plunge into grassy chasms right down to the valley below, but on this side a little path (the first one you will see after leaving the Coire Dubh Mor path) lures one forward over these plunging buttresses. You have to have the stomach for this sort of thing. I do not. However, it is possible to by-pass the 'enemy' by bum-sliding down the very steep but not dangerous screes on the north side descending almost down to the shores of the Lochan a' Choire Mhoir, and thence re-ascending by the steep slopes beyond the 'enemy', but such a loss of height and arduous manoeuvre may well put you off this idea. Better, perhaps, some other day, to approach the slopes from round the NW side as I will shortly describe if you don't fancy the traverse path, and return to climb the unnamed peak at 906608 and then the extensive flat top of Carn na Feola itself whose highest point, marked by a dilapidated cairn, lies at the extreme north point, before returning by the way you came.

The Coward's Way, or North West Passage   Distance 10 miles 16km Time 8 hours.

Leave your car at the Beinn Alligin car park (869576) and proceed NE up the main Coire Mhic Nobuil path. After 1¼ miles cross the river (Abhain Coire Mhic Nobuil) by the broad wooden bridge and follow the path north leading to the Bealach a' Chomhla between the Alligin Horns and Beinn Dearg. After ½ mile, *before* the wooden bridge over the Allt a' Bhealaich cross the ½ mile of rough terrain NE making directly for the extreme SW corner of Beinn Dearg at 887604. The purpose for taking this direction is two-fold. Firstly, it will bring you below the very steep SW slopes leading directly to the summit and you can at that moment decide whether you prefer to tackle these for a short, direct but potentially dangerous route to the top, as I have already described. If you choose this route it must be on your own responsibility, it is not my recommendation. Secondly, if you elect to proceed by way of the long, arduous, but safe northerly route it is better walking the mile up the valley on the Beinn Dearg side than on the side of the Horns of Alligin, providing you keep just below the zone of littered boulders at the foot of the mountain. Until you round the northern corner of the Stuc Loch na Cabhaig the going is fairly good if a little marshy in places, but once you round the corner all is changed and you are faced with rough heather, grass and boulder country set in an annoying series of up and down ridges. In order to avoid these as much as possible keep low so that you come round almost at the level of Loch na Cabhaig. The only compensation for the next miserable mile is that you are very likely to encounter large numbers of deer who will seem mildly surprised to see that you have chosen to take such a long-winded approach to Beinn Dearg's summit. Continue east until you reach the second burn descending from the mountainside, both streams being prominently crowned by high waterfalls. The grass slopes just beyond this second burn, though rough, are easy. Follow the stream up into the Choire Mhoir (marshy in places, nice sandstone slabs in others) and make for the NW corner of the Loch a' Choire Mhoir (898609) which is the key point for your final ascent to the summit. You are very unlikely to have to share this magnificent, vast and gloomy corrie with any other visitors. Above the NW end of the loch is a steep 400 foot grassy but partly scree and rock slope extending SW to the ridge which will lead you safely to the summit. Wet and sloshy to begin with the ground gets firmer and better as one ascends, requiring a bit of determination and some hard work but without any dangers or sense of exposure. As you climb you will gain magnificent retrospective views, looking down upon the 'enemy', that magnificent castle of rock which may previously have deterred you on an approach from the Carn na Feola side. You will also see the steep, arduous, but safe scree slopes below it, extending down to the shores of the loch, by which the 'enemy' can be turned on its north side on the Carn na Feola approach as a disheartening but safer alternative to tackling the more alarming southern traverse path.

Once on the ridge, which is broad, it is an easy stroll to the summit cairn. Only one flat lump of sandstone bars your way by straddling the ridge, but if you turn it by going round to its right (NE) side you are merely moving round above another part of the same grass slopes which you recently ascended. The tip of the summit cairn reaches above 3,000 feet, the cairn itself being situated on a broad grass and moss plateau. At the time of writing an old horseshoe stands at the tip of the cairn. Let it be he or she who removes it that has the bad luck. After resting and enjoying the fine views of the Alligin Horns, of Liathach and the full range of Beinn Dearg itself there are things you should do. Firstly, explore the SW edge of the summit plateau and peer down the steep gullies and precipitous rock cliffs which make a descent on this side potentially dangerous. Secondly, move north to the commencement of the narrow ridge joining the summit of Beinn Dearg with that of Stuc Loch na Cabhaig to the north-west. If you feel you can negotiate this ridge to reach its lowest point (at 893612) you will have a less arduous descent down easier slopes back to the Choire Moire.

I did not suggest you ascended this way in case you found you did not like this part of the ridge having then wasted considerable effort to reach it. From the summit plateau you are looking directly down at the worst thirty yards of it, where a small traverse path runs below (north-east) of the rocky crest, in some places protected by rock outcrops and at other times completely exposed to the precipices below. If you feel you can manage this section, the rest becomes somewhat less disconcerting as you move along the crest of a broadening ridge with occasional grassy platforms and some rocky obstacles requiring easy clambering but with some sense of exposure. If you do not fancy this airy ridge, which is mild compared with the traverse of the 'enemy' to the south, you will have to return to descend the steep slope by which you originally ascended. The sitting posture helps in places here if, like me, you are becoming ancient.

Verdict on Beinn Dearg

A fine rough mountain offering a variety of considerable challenges with but one Achilles heel in the defences of its main summit. For those who can handle steep slopes and narrow ridges and have the stomach for traversing the 'enemy' it offers a fine rough long and complicated high level walk but it is also worthy of the attention of any hill walker who is interested in more than just an easy day on the hills. Please remember that the north side of Beinn Dearg is out of bounds from September 1st to November 21st.

The northern face of Liathach and Am Fasarinen from Carn na Feola (Beinn Dearg).

N8: Baosbheinn 875m 2,868ft.

O.S. sheet 19. 12 miles 19.3km. 6 hours. Wading may be necessary.
(Map p.105)

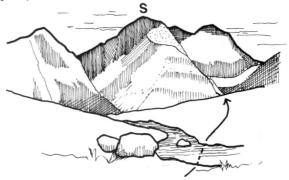

Baosbheinn from the NE. Having crossed the river (Abhainn a' Gharbh
Choire) as best you can, the summit (s) is most easily reached up the
northern slopes of the unnamed corrie (arrow). The peaks on either side
of the summit are daughter peaks of the same mountain.

Baosbheinn ('Booshven' or 'bershven', the wizard's or magic
mountain) is a long way from anywhere your car might care to go. It
looks beautiful from the south (eg. from Beinn Alligin) and gloomy
from the north, but the approach from the north is shortest and easiest
so that is what I will describe. As for Beinn an Eoin, this approach is
along the excellent 3½ mile track from Am Feur Loch, on the Kinlochewe to Gairloch road, to Loch na h-Oidhche. Baosbheinn offers a
long but rough up and down peak and ridge walk, but I will simply
take you on the highest summit. (Map p.105).

Leaving your car at the corrugated iron barn opposite Am Feur Loch
(at 857721) take the track south to Loch na h-Oidhche for 3½ miles
across magnificent scenery. The first glimpses of Baosbheinn's row of
peaks show it to be a long way away. At the stepping stones at 886676
follow the river upstream without crossing it; to the point where it
leaves the main river, the Abhainn a'Gharbh Choire (the river of the
black corrie) at 884676 and here you must cross, wading, except in
very dry weather. Once across, change your socks, and face the ½ mile
trek across rough ground, at first marshy and then rockstrewn, to reach
the unnamed corrie at 870660, which is the key to your final ascent to
the main summit. It is because of this 1½ mile traipse over rough

115

country and the much rougher and less pleasant ridge, that I place Beinn an Eoin above Baosbheinn in my order of recommendation for the modest hill walker. From the same point on the Loch na h-Oidhche track Beinn an Eoin is more quickly reached and the ridge more conducive to easy enjoyment.

Once you enter the corrie the ascent is up fairly easy grassy and rocky slopes and a final 60ft. easy scramble up the final slopes to the curved summit plateau, which has a fine cairn and is like a bowling green underfoot compared with the 1½ miles of rough terrain you have previously crossed. The views from the top, as usual, are magnificent, and NW and SE the humps and bumps of Baosbheinn's long ridge, along which a vestigial path threads its way, is available for exploration if you desire. I suggest that Beinn an Eoin is the better mountain for fell-mice, but fell-tigers prefer Baosbheinn.

N9: Meall a' Ghiubhais 878m 2,679ft.

O.S. sheet 19.

Beinn Eighe Nature Reserve Mountain Trail 550m 1,800ft.

Distance 2 ¹/₂ miles 4km. Time 4 hours.

Meall a' Ghiubhais ('Mel-a'-yuvay', the peak of the fir tree) is out of bounds to those wishing to respect the request of the Nature Reserve conservancy. It is adjacent (west) to the Nature Reserve's official Mountain and Nature Trails and we are asked in the guidebook, 'please keep to the trail, as animals will come to regard the presence of humans as quite normal and you will have a much better chance of close range observation'. Meall a' Ghiubhais has the easy slopes on its NW aspect, accessible (from reading the map) from the designated Mountain Trail at 987638, but out of respect for the request of the Nature Reserve to keep to the path, I have not attempted this particular summit. However, the shorter official Mountain Trail affords an excellent morning's or afternoon's expedition. Without specifically saying so, the earlier guidebook implies an anti-clockwise route by warning that 'the descent is very steep and rocky'. This is more a warning against high-heeled shoes and dancing pumps and need not alarm the hill walker. However, it seems much better to go *clockwise* up the 'steep and rocky' part first, since it is always easier to ascend than descend steepness, and then to enjoy the lovely views of Loch Maree, Gleann Bianasdail and Slioch on the longer easier descent down to the Coille na Glas Leitire. Otherwise, you have a long ascent up this steep sided valley, with no views ahead, and you will be over-occupied sliding down the rocks going down the steep part fully to enjoy the views of Loch Maree, if you go anti-clockwise.

Obtain a copy of the guidebook *(Beinn Eighe National Nature Reserve Glas Leitire Nature Trail)* from the Reserve's Visitor Centre at 022628, 1 mile north of Kinlochewe. The Centre is well worth a visit in its own right. A generous and well signposted car park by the loch-side at 002650, marks the commencement of both trails. You pass under the road. Send elderly or infirm relatives up the right fork in the path to enjoy the easy Nature Trail, and take the left fork if you plan to do the Mountain Trail yourself and agree, from my reasoning, that clockwise sounds more sensible. Just follow the path. It is delightful all the way and there are grand views of Beinn Eighe's rugged northern peaks from the high point at 994633. I strongly recommend this shortish expedition for the enjoyment it engenders and it is also a good way of finding out if friends, new to the business of hill walking, will be able to manage the bigger peaks.

SOUTHERN GROUP

S1: Beinn Damh 902m 2,960ft.

O.S sheet 24.   Total distance 5 or 7 miles, 8 or 11.3 km (main summit). Time 5 hours or 6 ¹/₂ hours.   (Map p.119)

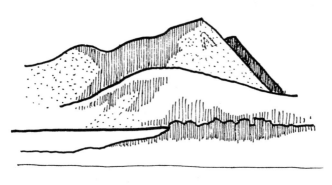

Beinn Damh from the Kishorn road.

Beinn Damh, seen from the summit of An Ruadh Stac, displays its main summit and impressive eastern precipices which are not seen from the road.

This mountain, whose true ruggedness is hidden from motorists, offers an easy ascent with some rough stuff at the top. There are two main summits on the mountain proper, the nearer and more accessible being some 120ft. lower than the more distant official summit, and also a subsidiary northerly outpost, the Sgurr na Bana Mhoraire ('sgorr-na-barna-voraire', his lordship's (the mountain's) consort), one short part of the ascent of which involves traversing a narrow slanting path on a steepish slope above crags.

In climbing Beinn Damh ('Ben-darv', the mountain of the stag), you can either opt for the higher more distant summit first and take the lesser on your way back, descending by the slopes of Craig na h-iolaire (C) for variation from your way of ascent:- safe and simple if you pick and choose your way, or climb the lesser peak first and then decide whether you have enough puff to do the main summit. I think it is nicer, in every way, to do the latter and my route, to the lesser summit first, minimises the amount of clambering you have to do over the piles of quartzite clinker which constitute its summit.

There is room to park three cars on the Shieldaig to Annat road just above the Loch Torridon Hotel, (whose gothic turrets are visible above the trees) on the right-hand side travelling from Shieldaig,

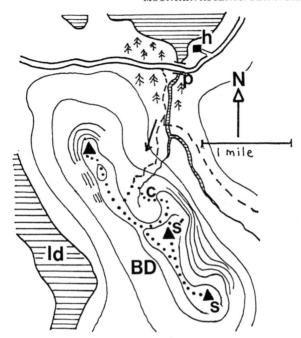

The routes to the summits of Beinn Damh (BD).
**Main summit (s), nearer summit (s′). There is room to park several cars
either side of the bridge above the Loch Torridon Hotel (h).
Loch Damh (ld). Craig na h-iolaire (c).**

either side of the bridge over the Allt Coire Roill at 887541 (p). Walk
back up the road towards Shielding for 70 yards and find the steep
track up the bank on the left-hand side which is at the commencement
of the path which ascends in the pine and rhododendron forest (a
beautiful walk, this, when the rhodos are out). As you climb for ½
mile the rhododendrons fade away, you cross two delightful tumbling
burns, and the roots of many of the trees become smaller and smaller.
Note, as you ascend, how the roots of many of the trees, which lie
under the path, are exposed. Wet exposed roots are, second only to ice,
the most slippery hazard one encounters when walking and are good
breakers of ankles. So, on your way down at the end of the day when
you are tired and relaxed, take care. As you near the upper limit of the
trees you are afforded a fine view of the 60 foot waterfall across the

119

chasm where the trees have been cleared. Some large boulders mark this spot but you will not miss it.

As you emerge above the tree-line, take the *right* fork in the path (although it is worth descending for 100 yards on the other, left-hand, path for a good view of the river as it tumbles downwards within its rocky chasm). Keep following the path as it, or rather you, ascend laboriously towards the big saddle which joins Beinn Damh proper to the Sgurr na Bana Mhoraire. The path enters a small scree shoot, so look for the little zig-zag path 15 yards up it to your right which ascends more easily in the stout clumps of heather. The shoulder is very broad and it is worth immediately walking SW across it, beyond its 'mid-point' cairn, to look down the very steep westerly scree slopes into Loch Damh below. You should now be at 876518. This shoulder and the main summit plateau are large and featureless, crags and steep slopes abounding; however, it is an easy mountain to get off by compass if you are misted out so you might consider your future tactics for this event at this juncture. The saddle top is featureless moorland and the path becomes vague as you move across it and begin to ascend in a SE direction.

As you pick up the path again it will lead you upwards towards the main peak (902m) above the stirrup mark and 1½ miles away. I suggest you leave it early at a convenient moment to ascend more steeply up grass slopes to your left in order to keep to the edge of the huge mountain bowl (contained in the left half of square 880510) which you will have seen and admired as you ascended to the saddle. Work your way round the very edge of the cliff of this bowl as far as you can go, that is to point 886513. You will note, during this manoeuvre, that you are walking pleasantly on grass and flat slabs of sandstone and avoiding the two hundred feet pile of quartzite rubble which constitutes the summit. Just before you reach the easterly crags ahead turn SSW to ascend steeply by clambering up the shattered lumps of quartzite, taking advantage of the numerous grass and moss patches. This way you are only 5 minutes from the top.

The delightful summit affords fine views, especially of the projecting crag of the 902m main summit SSE. To reach this, or to return home, descend first south down easy slopes of quartzite and grass. At the lowest point, if you wish to go home, move W and then NW keeping always to the grass slopes *below the piles of quartzite rocks* over which you have to clamber if you insist on following the line of cairns and thus traversing higher. In effect you are now moving from point 887505 back towards point 876515 where you commenced your ascent from the saddle. If, alternatively, you intend now to do *the main summit*, it is virtually always in view ahead, so just aim across the wasteland of quartzite towards it. The ridge leading to the summit cairn is not narrow (at least 8-10 feet wide) although it could be a trial in high winds. When you return from this summit, again keep as low as possible on the grassy plateau below the subsidiary summit as described above. The final descent back through the forest is always a delight even if your feet are throbbing, but watch out for those exposed roots.

BEINN LIATH MHOR, SGORR NAN LOCHAN UAINE, BEINN LIATH BHEAG AND SGURR DUBH.

This beautiful range of peaks, culminating in Sgorr Ruadh and Fuar Tholl to the south, form the eastern boundary of the southern Torridon peaks and their impressive backsides are well seen as one travels by road from Achanalt via Achnasheen towards Kinlochewe. Beinn Liath Mhor, Sgorr nan Lochan Uaine and Beinn Liath Bheag and Sgurr Dubh can most easily be climbed from the excellent stalker's path which goes south past the Ling (climber's) hut at the head of Glen Torridon at 957563. The modest hill walker will find it less taxing in all respects to tackle Sgorr Ruadh and Fuar Tholl from the south. Only hard walkers will think of doing the complete 8 mile ridge of summits in one go because of the many ups and downs that are involved. Beinn Liath Mhor, Sgorr nan Lochan Uaine (linked with Beinn Liath Bheag for a fuller expedition) and Sgurr Dubh done individually offer those of limited capacity separate excellent days out, and what lover of the hills could ever tire of treading and retreading

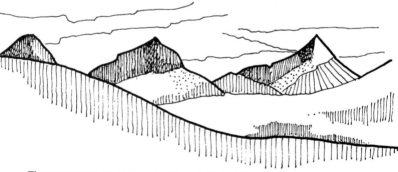

The eastern peaks of Glen Torridon. Left to right:- Sgorr nan Lochan Uaine, Beinn Liath Mhor and Sgorr Ruadh.

121

the beautiful Ling path? For each of these ascents leave your car at the head of Glen Torridon car park (957568). Proceed 100 yards down the road towards Kinlochewe and proceed south down the stalker's path at 960569 past Lochan an Lasgair and the Ling hut towards your selected mountain.

S2: Beinn Liath Mhor 925m 3,044ft. A Munro.

O.S sheet 25. Distance 8 ¹/₂ miles 13.8km. Time 7 hours.

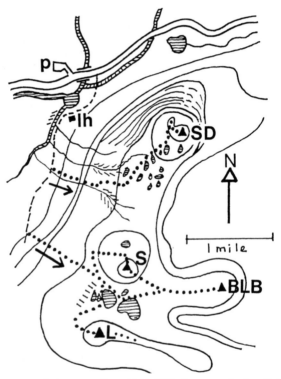

The recommended route to Sgurr Dubh (SD), Sgorr nan Lochan Uaine (S), Beinn Liath Bheag (BLB), and Beinn Liath Mhor (L). Glen Torridon car park (p), Ling Hut (lh).

Proceed up the Ling path almost to its end at 952539. Turn SE and ascend sloping ground, the first 200 yards of which are rough due to thick heather and burns. Aim more towards Sgorr nan Lochan Uaine (to point 964530) to avoid the inviting but often wet and slippery fairly steep slabs and terraces guarding the lochans to the right. This will also be your route of Sgorr nan Lochan Uaine. At the top of these slopes find your way to the lower of the two big, so called, 'green' (uaine) lochs. Pass south, between this and the tinier lochans to the west, and head straight up the grass and rock slopes to the obvious shoulder beneath the main (925m) summit of Beinn Liath Mhor (Ben-lia-vorr', the big grey mountain). As you begin this ascent, the summit towers threateningly above you and looks to be hours away but the actual ascent is easy all the way. Once you reach the saddle, it is an interesting ascent through great lumps of white quartzite rocks to the delightful summit which you share with its cairn. Beyond (east) is a somewhat narrow 1¹/₂ mile crest ridge which you can explore if you feel inclined and the views of Sgorr Ruadh's plunging precipices across the valley to the south will inspire a sense of awe in any sensitive breast. Return by your route of ascent or, if you are fairly energetic, take in the summit of Sgorr nan Lochain Uaine on your way down. Beinn Laith Mhor is connoisseur stuff and highly recommended; when you climb it you have Munro'd.

S3: **Sgorr nan Lochan Uaine**   860m   2,820ft. and
S4: **Beinn Liath Bheag**   800m   2,584ft.

O.S. sheet 25. Distance 7 or 9 miles, 11.3 or 14.5 km. Time 6 or 7 hours (Map p.122)

Ascend to the Lochan Uaine via the Ling path as described for the ascent of Beinn Liath Mhor (p122). Two hundred yards before you reach the lochan at point 963531, you will see to your left (north) a broad grassy and rocky couloir ascending obliquely slightly backwards (NNW), towards the ridge which then leads to the summit of Sgorr nan Lochan Uaine (the peak of the green lochan). This offers the easiest route of ascent but there are numerous alternatives which will all take you to the summit cone which stands majestically above you. Once you have attained the ridge aim straight ahead towards the summit. A direct ascent of the final 200ft. summit cone, however, lands you into an awkward final scree scramble. This can be avoided by first moving north and east to the left round the cone in order to reach and ascend by the easier slopes on its N and NW aspect. Note the delightful little unnamed lochan below you. The slopes here, below the summit, afford an easy and amusing little scramble up loose quartzite rocks, numerous mossy patches offering some relief from the rubble of small boulders as you ascend. In winter and early spring however, these N and NW slopes may be iced up and difficult to ascend without ice axe and crampons. The top is a generous moss-covered plateau with a dilapidated shelter cairn.

It is pleasant to return by the green lochans, at first descending by the moss and grass ridge east of the summit, negotiating occasional patches of quartzite scree as you go. Ahead, but 1¼ miles away, lies the rounded summit of Beinn Liath Bheag ('Ben-leea-veck', the little grey mountain) uniformly whitish-grey in appearance, being covered almost entirely by quartzite. However, the quartzite on this enticing little eminence consists of small pieces pressed hard into the ground and the going all the way to the summit is pleasant. As you approach, negotiating two rows of small sandstone cliffs, you will notice an isolated boulder of red sandstone some forty feet directly below the summit cairn standing at the head of a very short loose scree slope which is about the only loose stuff one has to encounter before reaching the top.

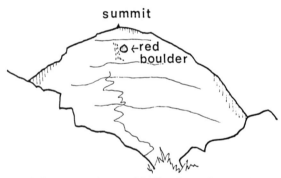

The summit boasts a cairn, and half a dozen large red sandstone boulders lie on the summit plateau, looking rather like stranded whales in the surrounding white quartzite. The Coire Beinne Leithe and views across it to the screes of Beinn Liath Mhor present a grim visage. The walk to Beinn Liath Bheag from Sgorr nan Lochan Uaine is so pleasant that I strongly recommend including this two thousand five hundred footer as part of your expedition. I do, however, advise against trying to link Sgorr nan Lochan Uaine with Sgurr Dubh two miles to the north, as the intervening ground is rough and complicated and may weary you, but for the young and fit there are no serious obstacles between these two peaks. In mist however, you could become lost in this terrain.

A return to the upper reaches of the Ling path, between the shattered western slopes of Sgorr nan Lochan Uaine and the three green lochans, either after descending the grassy ridge extending from the eastern end of its summit, or on your return from visiting Beinn Liath Bheag, is more pleasant and interesting than returning round the north side. The ground here is rough grass and sandstone with a few ups and downs. The lochans themselves are delightful and the summit of Beinn Liath Mhor to the south is impressive. After ascending the low sandstone cliff immediately beyond the last of the three main lochans, you are set to continue straight down the rough heather and boulder ridden slopes, that you previously ascended, to reach the Ling path. Deer abound in this region so please remember that there may be stalking in this part of the Coulin Estate in August, September and October.

S5: Sgurr Dubh 782m 2,564ft.

O.S. sheet 25. Distance 6 miles 9.7 km. Time 5 hours. (Map p.122).

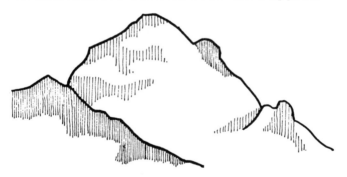

Sgurr Dubh from the Torridon road.

Sgurr Dubh ('Sgorr-doo', the black peak) is easily climbed, but the terrain is wild and rough. (Map p.122)

Proceed along the Ling path until you reach the third burn crossing (955550). Do not cross this, but follow its tumbling waters ESE towards the great chasm in the mountainside from which it emerges.

This leads you to the easiest part of the slopes which are barring your way to the long broad mountain ridge ahead. The great gully, which appears ominous from a distance, is a delightful place on close acquaintance, but as soon as you reach more steeply sloping ground, move away obliquely ENE to your left, above a small grassy promontory, and zig-zag your way up the heather, grass and rocky slopes, avoiding the odd patches of scree for greater comfort. This involves 250ft. of very easy scrambling and takes 20-25 minutes. When you reach the crest you enter a magnificently wild and grand scene of great chasms and rocky promontories, but the walk to the summit is easy as these features can all be enjoyed without having to be negotiated.

You will have noted from the map that you have ascended by the slopes between the river gully to the south and the commencement of Sgurr Dubh's rocky cliffs which extend for 2 miles almost to the road to the north. Note the point of your arrival on the crest for your return. A ridge 200 yards to the east at first obscures your views to the summit but once this is reached, the summit region remains in view all the way and you should aim directly for it keeping, in general, to the left of the numerous lochans and their rougher terrain. As you approach the formidable precipices ahead, veer to your left NNW up a grassy and rocky slope beneath the cliffs which by-passes this obstacle, which is not the true summit. As you round the corner at the top, the true summit declares itself and it is only a traipse across shattered quartzite scree slopes to reach the summit cairn. On your left you will have noticed a grassy subsidiary summit which is equally easily ascended. This is the knob which dominates the road as you pass the head of Glen Torridon. It is therefore worth a visit, for the two summits, so close together, could hardly be more different; the main summit a wilderness of shattered white quartzite scree and its little neighbour all grass and brown sandstone. Return by the route of your ascent for the easiest descent down the mountain slopes to the valley, employing occasional six-point contact to get you down the steeper bits. The wildness of the upper terrain, so quickly reached, and Sgurr Dubh's glowering dominance at the head of Glen Torridon make it a peak well worthy of your attention.

S6: **Beinn na h-Eaglaise** 737m 2,417ft.

O.S sheet 24/25. Distance 7 miles 11.3km. Time 6 hours. (Map p.128).

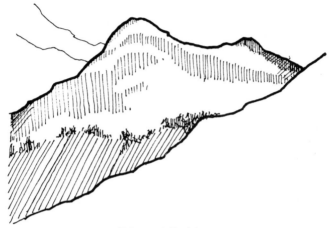

Beinn na h-Eaglaise.

Somewhat dwarfed by its bigger neighbour Beinn Damh, Beinn na h-Eaglaise ('ben-na-uggalish', the mountain of the church) is a charming little fellow whose top is well worth a visit when you feel like an easier day. Its north and east sides are well protected by rocky buttresses but the slopes on its southern and western sides are fairly easy with only minor obstacles which can be turned. A pleasant way of doing the mountain is to leave your car on the south side of the road above the Loch Torridon Hotel on either side of the bridge at 887541. Walk along the road west towards Shieldaig for 70 yards, to find the gate up in the bank on the left side, which gives access to the path which ascends in the rhododendron and fir tree wood for half a mile. This is the same route described for the climb up Beinn Damh (2) see map p.119. After emerging from the wood take the *left* fork in the path down to the river which has to be crossed. The path leads to suitable stones which can be used as stepping stones in dry weather but may be unsuitable when the river is in spate; in which case it is safer to wade further upstream where the river is wider and the bottom pebbly, rather than risk crossing at the narrower part where the water may be gushing over the stones.

An alternative is first to ascend up the forest track just beyond the

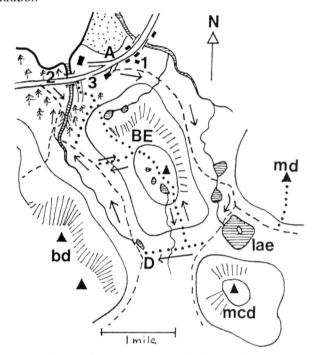

Suggested routes up Beinn na h-Eaglaise (BE).
1. As part of walk round the mountain from Annat (see Walk No.5).
2. A shorter and more direct ascent can be made up the path to Beinn Damh (bd). 3. (as an alternative to 2) avoids the river crossing.
Loch an Eion (lae), Meall Dearg (md), Maol Chean Dearg (mcd),
Drochaid Coire Roill (D).

bridge on the Annat/Torridon side at 889541 and thence diagonally upwards, climbing the bracken-covered slopes with the river away on your right, aiming for the break in the trees on the skyline. (3) See map above.

If you have crossed the river successfully, continue up the path for a further half mile. If, however, you have failed to get across, you will not want to go all the way down to the road in order to start again up the other side of the river which, being in a deep rocky ravine, cannot be crossed between these two points, so it is best to decide either to get your feet wet or to climb Beinn Damh, to your right, instead.

After half a mile or so leave the path to ascend grassy slopes on your left to reach the summit ridge of the mountain. If you have come up the bracken-infested slopes on the east side of the river, however, there is no need to find the path as you can continue ascending more or less direct to the summit ridge passing to the right (west) of the line of crags on the northern aspect of the mountain.

Having reached the summit, you can descend in a SSE direction in order to enjoy the cluster of fine lochans and thence, continuing south, down grass slopes, with some boulders, and then west to Drochaid Coire Roill (Bridge of the Corrie Roill) (D). From here the views to the east of Sgorr Ruadh and Beinn Liath Mhor and to the south of Maol Chean Dearg are very fine but most impressive are the easterly precipices of Beinn Damh which you can admire while you walk back for two miles NW along the path to bring you back to the river crossing at 885532. Even if you previously decided to ascend the mountain direct on the east side of the river, it is worth examining the river to see if you can cross it because the walk down the fir tree and rhododendron forest back to the road is far more pleasant than the free-ranging descent down the steep bracken slopes on the other side. If you decide not to cross the river (it is usually OK except in winter or high rains) retrace your steps up the path for ¼ mile to the old deer fence. If you then follow this across rough ground in a NE direction to a gap in the trees below you, it will direct you towards the bracken slopes which you previously ascended. Careful map reading and a compass bearing will assist you to do this manoeuvre correctly.

This expedition is, in fact, somewhat similar to Walk No.5 except that you go over the top of Beinn na h-Eaglaise instead of round it. The alternative fuller day is to combine the full circuit walk (1) with an ascent of the mountain from the south side as described in Walk No.5.

S7: Beinn Shieldaig 516m 1,693ft.

O.S. sheet 24. Distance 5 miles 8km, 5 hours or 6 miles 9.6km, 6¹/₂ hours. (Map p.131)

You will appreciate, from the details given above, that I have no right to include Beinn Shieldaig (the mountain of the herring bay) among ascents over 2,000 feet since it stands a mere 1,693 feet above Shieldaig bay. However, it is such a grand and rewarding little mountain that it certainly justifies its inclusion among the 'mountain ascents'

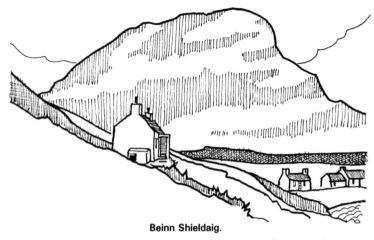

Beinn Shieldaig.

rather than among the 'high-level walks' since its fine summit ridge gives one the real feeling of being on a mountain top, the ridge being approximately three miles long and very good for walking. In contrast, Sgurr a' Ghaoiachain and Meall Gorm on the Applecross Peninsula, standing at 2,600ft. and 2,325ft. respectively, have, legitimately, to be included, because of their heights, but the first 2,000ft. of each may be climbed in your car simply by going by road up the Bealach na Ba.

Beinn Shieldaig has four distinct and cairned summits fairly evenly spaced. A shorter expedition is to ascend only the two higher ones at the mountain's NW end in order to look down onto the village of Shieldaig and take an unusual photographic view of it to show your friends. The longer trek is to walk the complete ridge from south to north taking in all four summits. Visitors staying in Torridon, Kinlochewe or Lochcarron may not feel tempted to travel to Shieldaig to climb this little mountain, but hill walkers staying in Shieldaig will surely feel its constant challenge. I will describe the ascent of the two highest and most northerly summits first.

Ascent of the two most northerly summits
Do not attempt to climb Beinn Shieldaig by way of the NW rocky precipices which immediately dominate the village, unless you are a very experienced scrambler. There are much easier slopes 1½ miles to the east (by the River Balgy) or on the west side above Loch Dughail ('lohh-dool'). *The Balgy ascent is the easiest (1).*

Park your car on the north side of the road 25 yards before the Balgy

130

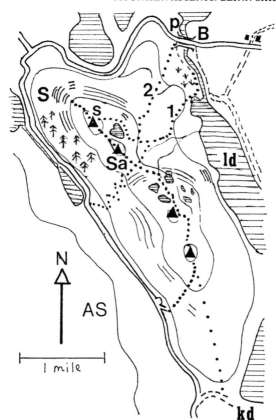

Beinn Shieldaig, showing the various pathless ascents described in the text. There are four distinct and cairned summits, separated into two pairs (N and S) by the main broad saddle (Sa). Balgy bridge (B), Loch Damh (ld), Kinloch Damh (kd), An Staonach - An Fur ridge (AS), Shieldaig village (S), Main summit (s).

bridge at 846544. Take the path running on the west side of the river, not the more popular path leading to the falls on the east side. Follow this somewhat muddy path to the 'jetties' at 851533 and then cross marshy ground SW to the little beach at 849532. Above you to the SW you will see the rough grassy and rocky slopes leading to an obvious low saddle (Sa) on the skyline which joins the two northerly and two

131

southerly summits. It is now a matter of free-ranging directly toward this saddle, ascending heather and grass slopes, initially somewhat steeply as you leave the beach (1). About two thirds the way up this slope you will have crags dead ahead on the skyline, and it is easier now to change direction diagonally to your right towards an obvious grassy gully (g) beyond the cliffs (going from point 842522 to 837524) to bring you onto the ridge at the large Loch nan Eun (loch of the bird), 835525.

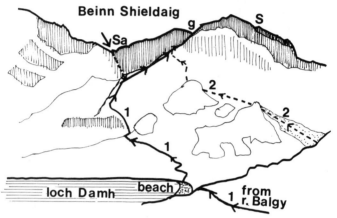

Ascent of the NE side of Beinn Shieldaig (alternatives). Summit ridge (s).

An even more direct route from the Balgy river road bridge may be taken (2). A direct (magnetic) bearing from the west end of the bridge (847544) of 200° will aim you across marshy and grassy ground towards a gently sloping rock-strewn couloir dead ahead. A vestigial path aims in this direction and helps a little if you can locate it. On surmounting the couloir keep ascending grassy and heather slopes, keeping to the right and working higher at every opportunity, until you are close under the rocky cliffs of the summit plateau and below the Loch nan Eun (see map). Then proceed horizontally in a S direction in order to round the end of the cliffs to join the grassy gully at 837524, and reach the summit plateau at the SE end of the Loch nan Eun, as described on the recommended route. Once you know the mountain this approach reduces the amount of rough heather and rocky terrain you have to ascend but the landmarks and one's sense of direction are less clear on a first ascent from this side.

Steep slopes run into Loch nan Eun on its SW side and it is pleasanter to stroll round the right-hand side (NE side) on the flat sandstone slabs before aiming directly for the most distant and main summit(S) (516m) at 828530. This reached, (it is prominently cairned) you will have to descend a series of large terraces in order to get better and better views of Shieldaig village, to a point where further progress is best avoided.

On your return you can now stay high on the ridge above Loch nan Eun to take in the subsidiary summit at 836524 and then continue down (south-east) to the lowest point of the saddle (839518) (↘) from where a steepish but safe descent through heather and large boulders to the slopes previously ascended takes one back to the Balgy river and thence to the road.

Four summit walk

Leave your car in Shieldaig and take Duncan MacLennan's white minibus from Shieldaig bus shelter adjacent to the Tigh an Eilean Hotel (leaves 10.15 a.m.* except Sundays) and ask him to put you down 3½ miles up Glen Shieldaig at or about 844488, which is beyond the terraced crags that extend for 1½ miles beyond Loch Dughail on the SW aspect of the mountain. The precise place is of no importance as the slopes beyond this point are progressively easier. You are commencing your ascent ¾ mile or more south of the first summit (439m). As you reach the very broad summit ridge fine views of the Beinn Damh appear. Turn NNW to reach the first cairned summit. This approach involves negotiating small transverse buttresses, finding easy grass slopes down them. The terrain is complicated and should be avoided in mist. A compass bearing (350° from the middle of the very broad ridge) will keep you on course for the first cairned flat-topped summit. From there descend 100 feet down slopes to the right or left, between crags, to reach the second summit visible ½ mile NNW, keeping rather to the right (east) than the left (west) by following the highest ground.

From the cairn of the second summit one looks NW across the lowest saddle towards the third and fourth summits, the first being 1 mile to the NW. However, when descending from the second summit, you should keep well to the right, going due north, rather than NW towards the next summit and passing to the right (east) of a largish triangular lochan which is shown on the map at 842516. From there continue again somewhat to your right (ie. due N) in order to reach the grass slopes to the east of a long rock buttress spread EW above the saddle. If you fail to do this it is of little consequence as the buttress will cause you to work your way to the right (east) to reach these grassy slopes, before you can descend, anyway. A move to your left (west) will bring you to further buttresses and steep slopes and should be avoided.

Once you have reached the lowest point of the saddle, cross the deer fence by the centrally placed high stile, to reach the penultimate and then the main summit (516m) at 829530. You must then descend three or four very broad ledges to obtain increasingly good views of Shieldaig village below. If you visit the beautiful Loch nan Eun on your return re-ascend the subsidiary summit before returning to the saddle. From there (840518) the quickest way back to Shieldaig is to descend by the heather and boulder slopes on the SW aspect of the mountain to the road, zig-zagging to avoid occasional rock buttresses. This side is steeper than the NE (Balgy) slopes previously described, as you may wish to do a bit of bum-sliding down the steeper heather slopes, but it is a safe and fairly easy route of descent, if a little tedious. Once you reach the road there is a 2 mile walk along the very pretty loch sides to Shieldaig village.

The Beinn Shieldaig ridge offers very fine and comparatively safe snow walking in winter.

S8:   Beinn Bhan and Carn Dearg   896m   2,939ft.

O.S. sheet 24.   Distance 5¹/₂ miles 8.8km.   Time 4 hours. (Map p.135).

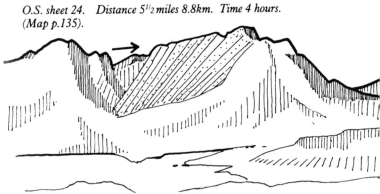

The Beinn Bhan massif from Bad a' Chreamha.
The route to the main plateau is via the narrow connecting ridge at the head of the Coire nan Arr. (→).

Beinn Bhan ('Ben-varn', the white mountain) is a huge plateau massif straddling the eastern boundary of the Applecross peninsula from north to south. A visit to its five easterly corries (there are actually six if you include the most northerly Coire Gorm Beag) has already been suggested (Walk No.4). A relatively narrow col (the Bealach nan Arr, pass of the ladder) joins Beinn Bhan to the 'mainland' plateau; otherwise it is generally surrounded by precipices, steep slopes and a narrow ridge except to the N. The col is 1¼ miles from the summit and the summit plateau is rough and featureless but the walking is good up there. For this reason this summit should not be visited if

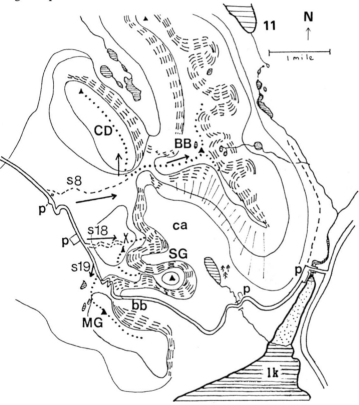

The Bheinn Bhan massif comprising Bheinn Bhan (BB), Carn Dearg (CD), Sgurr a' Ghaoiachain (SG) and Meall Gorm (MG). Bealach na Ba (bb), Corrie nan Arr (ca), Loch Kishorn (lk) and Loch Lundie (ll). Parking places at (p), and at (p⁀) (one car only). Suggested routes shown by dotted lines. (Ascents S8, S18 and S19).

mist or low cloud threatens unless you are expert in using a compass, otherwise you will find it very difficult to locate the way off if you cannot see. However, in clear conditions there are no problems.

A good stalker's path leads across the vast Coire nan Cuileag, commencing at 764437. There is just room to park one car on the W side of the road at this point (p). If you have come over the Bealach na Ba it is about 100 yards beyond the hairpin bend at 765436 and just beyond a white triangular passing sign. If you are coming up the road from Applecross it is on the right-hand side just before this sign. You will not see the commencement of the stalker's path which has been obliterated. Cross the grass and boulder verge (east) for 50 yards and you will find the path which runs just below the ruins of the shieling marked on the map at 764437. After a mile the path becomes indistinct where it goes up a gently rising grass strip. Keep your eye open for cairns, but if you lose the path no matter, you will be free-ranging soon enough. Just keep going towards the lowest point between the south end of Carn Dearg and the most northerly spur of Sgurr a' Ghaoiachain at 784444. At this point some cairns lead you to the left (north-east) towards higher ground. Ignore them; they are not helpful. Aim for the *lowest* part of this saddle, across rather rough, boulder-ridden ground, and as the Coire nan Arr begins to come into view you will see the path starting up again the other side of a small peat bog which is easily crossed at this point. This path takes you across to the Bealach in a traverse some 60 feet below the crest on an easy safe slope. The cairns which lead you to the higher ground simply compel you, in due course, to climb down again to this lower level in order to cross the Bealach itself. The col is very wide. The ascending ground on the other side is littered by sandstone rocks in a chaotic arrangement and achieving the main summit plateau depends on ascending half a mile of this rough ground, but a large number of small cairns, placed every 10-15 yards or so, lead one easily through this labyrinth. A large cairn marks your exit from this section and it is worth looking back at this as you proceed ENE towards the summit so that you can identify it on your return.

Some cairns lead across higher rockier ground but it is rather easier walking to keep a little below this broad flat ridge to the right (south). A final insult before you reach point 896m, where there is a large shelter cairn, is a descent of 50ft. and a scramble up a scree covered slope but a charming little lochan to your left is worth noting and visiting on your return. The sudden views from the summit down the east precipices into the Coire na Poite are dramatic and make this fairly easy ascent more than worthwhile. You are now on a huge plateau which you can explore at leisure, but your only easy or safe way off is back to the Bealach. Precipices or steep scree slopes surround you on all sides except to the far NW and the narrow ridge to the summit above Coire na Feola and Coire Each which requires some scrambling and a head for heights.

An alternative to walking as far as the summit of Beinn Bhan, after crossing the Coire nan Cuileag, is to ascend up the safe but adventurous ground to the *summit of Carn Dearg (645m 2,115ft.)*. The climbing of either Beinn Bhan or Carn Dearg is made easier by the fact that you are already at 1,400 feet when you park your car at 764437.

S9/10: Sgurr a' Gharaidh and Glas Bheinn
720m 2,361ft. 711m 2,332ft.

O.S. sheets 24/25. Distance 5 or 8¹/2 miles 8 or 13.8km.
Time 4¹/2 or 6¹/2 hours. (Map p.138).

Sgurr a' Gharaidh and Glas Bheinn from the Glen Shieldaig road.

Sgurr a' Gharaidh ('Sgorr-a-yaray', the peak of the beast's den), faces you as you drive S along Glen Shieldaig towards Kishorn. Glas Bheinn ('glass-ven', the grey mountain) dominates the village of Lochcarron. All tops in this region offer fine views of the surrounding mountains, but I suggest that Glas Bheinn is not a summit one should place high on one's list of planned ascents. However, as an extension to the ascent of Sgurr a' Gharaidh, which is a delightful expedition, Glas Bheinn is worth considering, approaching it from the W after climbing the former summit.

137

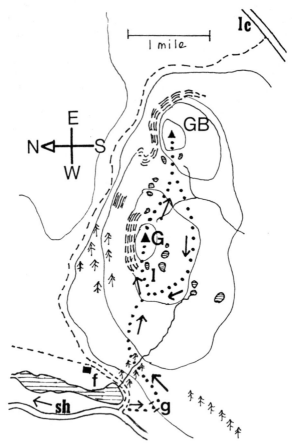

Ascent of Sgurr a' Gharaidh (G) and Glas Bheinn (GB) from the track to Glasnock Farm (f). You can leave your car just beyond the farm track (p). Lochan Meall na Caillich (l), Shieldaig to Kishorn road (sh), Lochcarron road (lc). Fence gate (g).

Leave your car on the Shieldaig/Kishorn road above Loch an Loin, just before the track leading to Glasnock Farm, at 853447: 100 yards down this track take up the earthy path going to your right, due south, and proceed for ½ mile. You are crossing farmland and you will see, above you to your left (south) a gate in the sturdy wire fence enclosing the farmland. By taking this route you can pass through the gate instead of trying to clamber over the fence and risk damaging it. Once through the gate turn NE towards the summit and the small gorge containing the sizeable burn which cascades down towards the loch. The slopes all the way to the summit are easy and you will, in the earlier part of your ascent, be negotiating very pleasant terraces of protruding rock. Fairly soon, as you ascend, the summit of Sgurr a' Gharaidh will pass out of sight. It is worth taking a direct compass bearing (94°) while it is still in view as you may easily lose your sense of direction once the summit has vanished from sight. This can save you unnecessary walking and waste of time as you can check your direction at regular intervals from your compass setting.

The gorge containing the stream is delightful and easy to cross in most places and this is followed quickly by the quartzite terraces. In due course you will emerge from these and find yourself on the edge of a somewhat gloomy corrie containing the lochan Meall na Caillich. You will 'pick up' an old fence coming up on your left if you are on route, but still the summit is out of sight. Minor humps can be surmounted or avoided by going round to the right of them and in due course the summit, guarded by a spider-shaped scree slope, comes into view. It is a simple scramble to the top but the worst of the scree can be avoided by traversing across its lower slopes to the right and thence up grass and rock gullies to the summit.

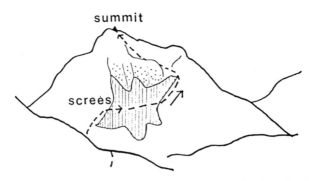

From the summit you will see the summit of Glas Bheinn 1¾ miles due E. To reach it you must descend 400ft. and re-ascend 370ft. so you can decide whether or not you feel this is worth the effort. An elliptical route, direct to the summit returning below and S of the summit of Sgurr a' Gharaidh saves you the task of re-climbing the higher peak on your way down. Thereafter, a descent approximately on the bearing 274° (directed at the prominent white house at Couldoran below) will bring you back approximately by the route of your ascent.

S11/12 Sgorr Ruadh and Fuar Tholl
960m   3,142ft.   907m   2,974ft.

O.S. sheet 25. Distance 7 or 9 miles 11.3 or 14.5km. Time 7-8 hours. Wading may be necessary.   (Map p.142).

These are the fine mountains standing above Achnashellach and the attainment of their summits is not difficult at the cost of a bit of hard work, but the ascent is accompanied throughout by plenty of drama. If you climb Sgorr Ruadh ('sgoorr-rua', the red peak) by the route I suggest you will be only half an hour from the summit of Fuar Tholl ('Fua-howl', the cold hollow) during your descent, so it is worth considering including both summits in one good day's outing, but I will also describe a separate and alternative route for Fuar Tholl. Although Sgorr Ruadh can be reached from the north, the distance is considerably longer and the ascent rougher and steeper, and I therefore recommend an ascent from Achnashellach station.

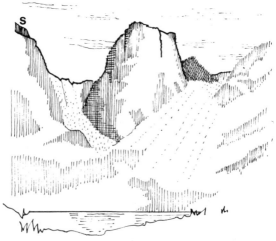

The cold hollow of Fuar Tholl and the impressive Mainreachan buttress (centre). Summit at (S).

Ascent of Sgorr Ruadh and Fuar Tholl or Sgorr Ruadh alone

You may not take a car up to Achnashellach station as the road up to it is private and says so. There is however, adequate parking space on the south side of the main road or on the grass to the E of the British Rail sign at 005484.

Proceed on foot up the private drive to Achnashellach station (the station of the field of willow). This must be one of the world's smallest stations set in an enchanted place in lush woodland, with the station-master's cottage and beautiful garden behind the platform and the towering cliffs of Fuar Tholl above and to your left. A delightful and adventurous stalker's path will take you for 2¾ miles right up to the Bhealaich Mhoir ('veallahh-voir', the big pass) the key to your ascent. Cross the railway line at the W end of the platform and pass through the wide iron gate on the opposite side. Proceed up the broad drive in the wood for 30 yards.

Turn sharp left where your track joins the main forestry track and proceed for ¼ mile until you come to the new gate across it. Pass through the pedestrian swing-gate portion and continue up the track for another 500m or so. A side path to your left then leads you through a new deer fence to the main mountain path.

Sgorr Ruadh from Coire Lair.

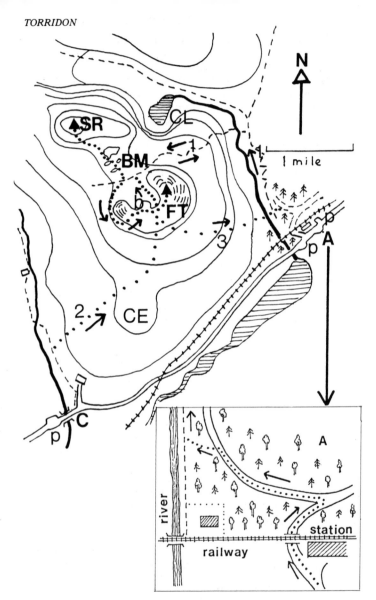

The first fifty yards of the path, after you have joined it, has marshy patches, but once you have crossed the wooden bridge it chirps up and gets better and better as you emerge from the forest and ascend with the cliffs of Fuar Tholl towering above you on the left, but separated from you by the deepening gorge of the River Lair.

As you emerge into the great Corrie Lair you will be impressed by the slopes and cliffs of Fuar Tholl, Sgorr Ruadh and Beinn Liath Mhor which confront you. Watch out for the cairn marking the branch path to the left (at 991502) which will lead you down to the river and thence for an easy ascent of 1½ miles to the top of the Bhealaich Mhoir. This river often requires wading but in drier weather one can be lucky by jumping across to serrated, and therefore not slippery, stones which may be just out of the water. The best place for this is where the path on the opposite side descends to the river. If you cannot cross dry-shod here you will simply waste your time if you search up and down stream for somewhere better. However, if wading is necessary, it is easier 10-15 yards downstream from this point where the river is wider and the bottom pebbly and more even.

As you approach the top of the Bhealaich, Fuar Tholl, the cold hollow, the Mainreachan buttress, and daunting screes leading to the summit ridge command attention. This will be your route of ascent of Fuar Tholl on your way back from Sgorr Ruadh, but do not be alarmed. I hate scree, but the threat of these screes is a sham, and this scree ascent, dominated by the precipices of Fuar Tholl and the Mainreachan buttress, is not very steep and surprisingly easy. You may have decided that Fuar Tholl alone is to be your target after all, but I will defer discussing the best route up Fuar Tholl until I have described a route to the summit of Sgorr Ruadh.

You have ½ mile of the Bhealaich to traverse from SE to NW. This is a complex and pathless terrain riddled by lochans, gullies and small precipices, which it is a minor adventure to cross. It is best to keep on the path to somewhere near its highest point and then launch yourself NNW towards Sgorr Ruadh, which is always in view, finding your way round the various obstacles thrown up against you. Once you reach the very fine large Loch a' Bhealaich Mhoir your troubles are over. Pass either east or west of this and proceed directly NW to the summit enjoying yourself by zig-zagging in order to turn the little

---

S11, S12 (1) Ascent of Fuar Tholl (FT) and Sgorr Ruadh (SR) from Achnashellach Station (A), via Coire Lair (CL) and the Bhealaich Mhoir (BM).
(2) Alternative route to Fuar Tholl from Coulags (C). Carn Eididh (CE) Mainreachan buttress (b).
(3) An alternative, tedious but practical, descent from Fuar Tholl to Achnashellach. Car parking (p).

buttresses and gullies arrayed against you. The climb to the summit cairn is half a mile and 900 feet so it takes a bit longer than one imagines. The summit shelter cairn stands as though on the very prow of a great ship and the views are spectacular.

In spite of the complexity of the terrain of the Bhealaich, this is an easy peak to get off by compass if misted out as your bearing is at right angles to the well-established path at the south end of the Bhealaich at which you are aiming. I speak from personal experience. In spite of the many deviations you have to make the slopes are safe on either side of this broad plateau and if you hold to your bearing as well as you can, you will inevitably come to this broad path at some point. This will take 1¼ hours or so from the summit under these conditions, and very nice it is to find it again, to be led by it back down into the Coire Lair and below the clouds.

Descending from Sgorr Ruadh you will regain the path crossing the south east end of the bhealaich near its highest point (969494, route 1A).

If you have planned to climb Fuar Tholl only ascend nearly to the highest point of the path and proceed SW across grass and sandstone (route 1). Routes 1 and 1A join at the foot of the quartzite scree slope beneath Fuar Tholl's un-named most westerly buttress. The plunging cliffs above may cause you some anxiety. In fact this popular route to the summit goes round the W and S side of the mountains across and up easy safe slopes. Look for a faint path going diagonally up the scree to your right (W). It starts about 50 yards E of the edge of the bhealaich

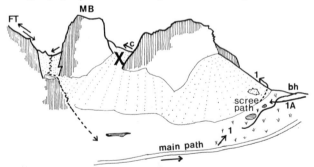

Ascent of Fuar Tholl (FT) by the indistinct path across screes round the back (SW) of the mountain (1), or after descending from Sgorr Ruadh via the Bhealaich Mhor (bh) (1A). Recommended descent by the easy screes between Fuar Tholl summit (FT) and the Mainreachan buttress (MB). N.B. The screes W of the Mainreachan buttress (X) are steep.

opposite the most westerly small lochan below the scree slopes. It diagonals off to the right at no more than 20° to the horizontal. *It does not ascend at all steeply.* Although indistinct it will lead you most easily round the side of the mountain, first across quartzite scree and then across slopes of sandstone boulders and grass. If you lose the path there are no dangers but your traverse will be rougher. You will reach a 30 foot wide grass and moss slope. Ascend this directly up the mountain side to reach the crest of the ridge just W of the Mainreachan buttress (C). There are fine views back across the valley to Maol Chean Dearg and An Ruadh stac.

Once you have gained the crest (C) turn right (East) to reach the cairned summit of the Mainreachan buttress (MB). The precipices to the W, N and E make this a dramatic viewpoint. From the buttress proceed along the ridge ESE to the low point between it and Fuar Tholl's main summit. At the very lowest point a cairn, and worn ground, mark the place from which to descend the screes below on your way down. Ascend the slope on the opposite side (NE) to gain the summit of Fuar Tholl itself (907 m. 2,974 ft.).

Redescend SW to the cairn at the lowest point of the ridge (974488) and gird yourself for a descent of the screes. Proceed N over the lip of the slope exactly at the lowest point marked by the cairn. I am not fond of scree but this slope affords a pleasant descent. Wide and not too steep, the fine scree at the centre, which the path follows, is set in a kind of mountain marzipan (dustier in dry weather, better when moist) and adheres well. Within the embrace of the cold-hollow and surrounded by plunging precipices, only the very timid will fail to find this quite easy descent exhilarating.

Halfway down the slope you will reach a grassy platform. Proceed to your left (W) to avoid buttresses and to descend the slightly steeper slopes below. Keeping between the edge of the scree adjacent to the Mainreachan buttress on your left and the rock and grass slopes on your right makes this part of the descent easier. At the bottom cross pleasant grassland, with a lochan to your left, to regain the main bhealaich path which you first ascended, to return to Achnashellach.

Warnings

i   There is always a risk of dislodging rocks on scree slopes to the detriment of those below you. The generally fine nature of the scree at the centre of this slope makes dislodgement unlikely, but a bunched party will be less at risk than a straggling one when descending these slopes.

ii   Unless you are adequately experienced avoid this descent when the hollow is filled with snow.

If you prefer not to descend the scree slopes you can either return to the bhealaich by your route of ascent, or make your way SE picking the easiest contours, down the rough grassy slopes above Sgurr a' Mhuilinn (986484) and thence ENE to reach and wade the river, after it has emerged from its gorge, at 998486, and thence regain the path in the woods on the other side. This descent is rough and tedious but offers a practical and safe route off the mountain (Route 3).

Ascent from Coulags and descent via Achnashallach **9 miles 14.5km. 7¹/₂ hours.** *Route 2.*

Fuar Tholl can be climbed by means of a long rough moorland walk from Coulags (Route 2). Leave your car just W of the bridge at MS (957451) and proceed up the path which ascends the Fionn-abhainn valley (marked by a sign:- PUBLIC RIGHT OF WAY TO TORRIDON). After ¾ mile the grass slopes to your right become easier. Chose a suitable place to leave the path and endure 400 foot of slimy grassy ascent to reach the pleasant moorland slopes above. A mile walk NE will bring you to the broad saddle between Fuar Tholl and Carn Eididh (973478). Ascend almost due N up the grassy slopes above you to the ridge between the 907m. summit and the Mainreachan buttress. Turn right (NE) to gain the summit cairn.

You can return either direct to Coulags, following the route of your ascent, or make the long round trip via Achnashellach, which makes for an enjoyable expedition for a long summer day. I suggest you descend the screes between the main summit and the Mainreachan buttress as already described, to reach the path on the Bhealaich Mhoir and follow this path (E) back to Achnashellach. When you reach the road at Achnashellach you will be 3¾ miles from Coulags. This is a pleasant road walk by the shores of Loch Dughail and Balnacra. One solution is for the fittest and fairest member to leave the others, with the rucksacks, to rest by the loch side and, thus unencumbered, be more favoured for a roadside lift back to the car at Coulags.

S13/14   Maol Chean Dearg and Meall nan Ceapairean
933m   3,060ft. and 670m   2,196ft.

O.S. sheet 25.   Distance 12 miles.   Time 8 hours.   (Map p.148).

Maol Chean Dearg ('Mel-hhin-jerrag', the bare red hill) is set deep in the southern Torridon group and there is a 4-5 mile hike to reach it from the south or the north. Approached from the north it is seen as a

Maol Chean Dearg from the Annat path. The recommended route to the summit is round to the right and from the other side.

big, bare, steep, scree-ridden and unfriendly lump. Meall nan Ceapairean ('myowl-nan-keeperun') from the north, is a mere adjunct to big brother, but from the south, approached from the Fionn-abhainn valley, its summit hides behind impressive cliffs and offers a worthwhile ascent for an easy day. Both summits are nearer the Loch-carron/Achnashellach road than Torridon, but the extra mile and a half required, being on a good path, hardly justifies the drive right round to the south for those staying at Shieldaig, Annat or Torridon.

The key for both ascents is the high pass (bealach) between Maol Chean Dearg and Meall nan Ceapairean, from point 931488. *To reach this from the south* take the path from Coulags (958451) going N up the Fionn-abhainn valley, and after 2½ miles take the steeply ascending left-hand path up to the bealach. *From the north take the path from Annat* (commencing at 894544, sheet 24) to Loch an Eion. Continue on this path SSW passing right round Maol Chean Dearg in order to reach its easier southern flank. It is a long way. As you ascend to the bealach, with Loch Coire an Ruadh-stac on your right, the wildness of the scenery and the great northern cliffs of an Ruadh-stac will impress you. Once at the highest point the mountain ascents can begin.

Meall nan Caepairean demands only a pleasant saunter up easy grass and rocky slopes to its summit from this point and you will hardly want to walk all the way from Torridon in the north just to do this. But from Coulags this makes for a pleasant and easy day out. Steepish, but not dangerous, quartzite scree slopes defend Maol Chean Dearg on the opposite side and a brisk scramble to the mountain's SE shoulder is required using, or ignoring, the zig-zag path up them as you wish. This is a rough but safe bit as long as you keep away from the steeper gullies to your right. This climb will bring you to point 930492. Thence proceed for ¾ mile NW to the summit, losing a little height before finally ascending the easy but chaotic rubble of

147

sandstone guarding the summit. Here there is a large summit shelter
cairn which can be seen when the mountain is viewed from the north.
It takes me four hours to reach this point from Annat and I am tired,

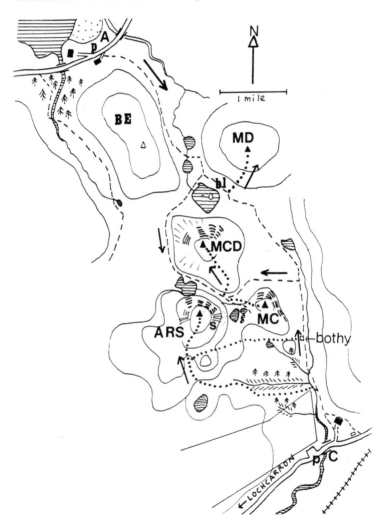

but the magnificent views and the feeling that one has surmounted this formidable-looking monster are adequate reward for the effort involved. Fell tigers will tell you about all the easy ways you can get directly down to Loch Coire Fionnaraich and the Bealach na Lice but, if you are not exhausted, you will want to 'pick off' the summit of Meall nan Ceapairean before you return to Coulags or Annat. Also, for those of modest experience, and for safety's sake, I suggest you descend by the route of your ascent. This is a fairly arduous but worthwhile outing, converting a hostile-looking giant into an old friend, and a Munro to boot.

S15: Meall Dearg 650m 2,132ft.

O.S. sheet 25. Distance 10 miles 16km. Time 5 hours. (Map p.148).

This pleasant little eminence is the soft option to climbing Maol Chean Dearg. The two summits face each other across the Bealach na Lice ('Bealuhh-na-Lihh', the pass of the flat stone). Leave your car at Annat and proceed up the stalker's path which commences at 894544 (sheet 24), as for the walk to Maol Chean Dearg. Just before the Loch an Eion, take the left-hand path, passing on the north side of the loch to the summit of the bealach. From there, free-range NNE up 700ft. over easy but rocky and grassy terrain for half a mile to the summit which has a small walker's cairn on it. You can get off Meall Dearg on most sides but there are some buttresses and a return via the path over the Bealach na Lice offers a simple safe retreat. Meall Dearg, of course, means the red hill.

Maol Chean Dearg (MCD).
Use the long but good paths from Annat (A) in the north, or Coulags (C) in the south to climb this mountain and its little neighbour Meall nan Ceapairean (MC) from the bealach between Maol Chean Dearg and An Ruadh-stac (ARS)

An Ruadh-stac (ARS)
The south ridge to the summit of this mountain is the easiest and safest (see p.156 for more detailed map).

Meall Dearg (MD) can be ascended from the path over the Bealach na Lice (bl). Car parking (p). Beinn na h. Eaglaise (BE).

S16: Beinn a' Chlachain and Meall an Doireachain (Applecross)
626m   2,053ft.

O.S. sheet 24. Distance 6-10 miles 9.7-16km. Time 4-6 hours. (Map p.151).

Beinn a' Chlachain and Meall an Doireachain from Applecross.

The ascent of these heights, above the Applecross valley, is more a high moorland walk than a mountain climb, but good in dry weather, and although more dramatic peaks are likely to command your attention first, this plateau of linked mountain tops offers a good day out with magnificent views of virtually the whole length of Skye throughout. The group is situated on the NW side of the River Applecross valley (summit at 724491) and could well be called the Heights of Applecross. The named tops, Beinn a' Chlachain (mountain of stones) and Meall an Doireachain ('mel-an-de'rehhan', hill of the copse) do not have cairned summits but there are cairns at 709469 and at the unnamed highest point at 724491 (626m). I would like to suggest three ways you might care to enjoy these heights.

---

1. Ascent of main summit and return   (4 hours, 6 miles)

Park your car at the generous roadside parking space at Cruarg, two hundred yards W of the white cottage (705457). Join the old coastal track going W above the road and use it to get beyond the rather steeper slopes immediately above Cruarg itself. After ¼ mile, make a 2¾ mile bee-line NE up to summit 626 (724491). It is rough for the first 200 feet and then as you get higher the grass and heather get

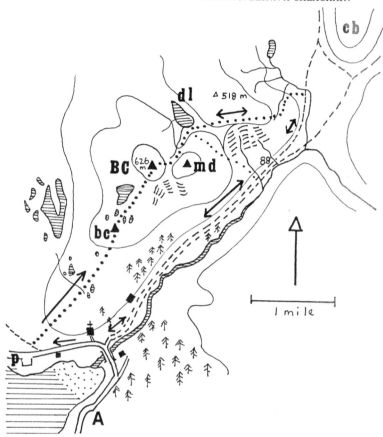

The ascent of Beinn a' Chlachain (BC) and Meall an Doireachain (md).
Return, or complete a circular walk by descending and returning down
the Applecross Estate road. Applecross village (A). An Dubh-loch (dl),
Croic Bheinn (cb). Parking area (p).

shorter and the going is good, with numerous lochans to enchant you
on your way. First you will encounter an elegant cairn at 709469. This
stands out prominently on the skyline when you return from Beinn a'
Chlachain and will be the point to aim for on your descent. A hundred
yards or so beyond the cairn you will encounter an escarpment of

151

rocky cliff which extends SE for ¾ of a mile from the southern tip of Loch nan Eun (705476). It is thirty feet high and easily negotiated either by slithering down numerous grassy gaps in the cliff or by turning the whole rampart by going a little to the right (north-east), where it peters out. Below this cliff you will find the first cluster of small lochans at 710470. There are no further obstacles between here and the summit point, and this obstacle is a trivial one. Beinn a' Chlachain is a stony place, as its name denotes, but these are sandstone slabs, good for walking. The main summit ridge lies ahead and it is a good idea to use your compass on a single direct bearing from the moment you leave the old track to keep yourself on the most direct and therefore shortest route. After Beinn a' Chlachain you will pass a large unnamed lochan on your left (719485) where I have seen a pair of black-throated divers. This whole area is a little visited wilderness so the chance of seeing wildlife is good. I saw my first eagle in the valley just beyond the 626m summit, which is marked by a large circular cairn sheltering a 'trig' point. A good spot for eating a sandwich, the rough and rounded top of Meall an Doireachain may tempt you before you descend by the route of your ascent, enjoying the fine views of the Cuillin, the Storr, the Quirang and of the island of Raasay as you go.

2.   *A round walk and a more adventurous day*   (10 miles, 6 hours)

Leave your car near the entrance to the private road into the Applecross estate (714457). First visit the simple but very delightful adjacent chapel. Then proceed NE for 4 miles up the road (through the estate) which becomes a track, and then a path, running parallel to the River Applecross to your right. Keep an eye out for deer. Keep to the left fork at point '88' (see OS map), with Croic-bheinn ahead. Just before the river crossing at 754504 turn SW, up rough but easy slopes to reach the flatter ground beneath Meall na Fhuaid (518m). A stream and gully commencing at 750505 offer a pleasant and easier ascent. (You can, however, shorten this initial manoeuvre by 1¼ miles if you prefer to ascend directly up the steeper rougher and relentless slopes below Meall an Doireachain leaving the path at 744487. Ascend to the right of the deep gully, crowned by a waterfall at its top, which cleaves the full length of these slopes). By either route you will attain the flattish ground under (south-east) Meall na Fhuaid (518m). From here on the numerous mountainous lumps and bumps can be very confusing so that careful map reading, supported by a compass bearing, is necessary. This area is too remote and complicated to be attempted in mist. The key to the easiest ascent to 626m summit is the southern shore of the sizeable An Dubh-loch (the black loch) at 734499. Follow the little stream which descends between the 626m summit (to the right) and Meall an Doireachain (to the left) up rough but easy ground. Near the top of this little valley veer to the right (west) up steeper ground to gain the summit shelter cairn (626m).

From the summit a beautiful downhill walk to Cruarg follows, past numerous lochans, with glorious views of Skye and glimpses of the wooded Applecross valley to your left. A compass bearing is useful to help you reach the old track half a mile *west* of Cruarg at about point 701457, where the final descent is less steep. The rocky escarpment which extends SE from Loch nan Eun is easily surmounted by scrambling up one of the grassy breaks in its defences, or by going to the left (east) where it peters out altogether. When you reach the old track follow it E until it joins the road to Applecross and thence along the road for ¾ mile to where you left your car.

3. *For compass practice on a misty day*

It is essential that hill walkers should be efficient and confident compass users, since a mist-out may catch one unexpectedly in high places if the weather changes. The problem for the occasional hill walker is lack of practice. The relative flatness of this terrain, the safe easy slopes in a SW and W direction and the fact that a compass bearing anywhere between these points will bring one back to the old track or new Applecross road, plus the remote wildness of the area can afford a safe but real exercise in the use of the compass in rough terrain. Best to go in a two- or three-some in case of a twisted ankle. Take torches and whistles and stick together. Park your car at Cruarg and ascend W on the old track for ½ mile as described on p.150. If cloud is down below 1,000 feet the terrain above looks steep, black and gloomy. Ignore this sham. Set your compass for one of the lochans and go to it. The reliable use of a compass requires always that you know where you are as well as where you want to go, so draw your route in pencil on the map as you proceed. Confirming that you have actually arrived at the described destination is necessary before proceeding, by bearing, to the next. With lochans this relates to shape and size. So measure accurately from the map the size of the lochan you should be at before proceeding. If you cannot, at least, find the big Loch nan Eun (loch of the bird) by compass in mist you should not be going onto mountains. This is a lovely area to be in in mist, full of mystery and magic, and I have used it for compass practice and an enjoyable morning out. The only hazard is the heart-stopping one when grouse suddenly take off from beneath one's feet, shattering the eerie silence by their noise. If you do get completely lost, just set your compass SSW or due W (according to where you think you are) for the quickest return to the road. But any bearing between these two points will get you to the road safely and you should be, apart from incidental ups and downs, *descending* all the way.

Restrict yourself to going only about 1½ miles, as far as the first chain of lochans which extend SE from Loch nan Eun, and descending the 30 foot rocky escarpment in mist to reach these will add a little frisson to your adventure. But however complex the terrain may seem under these conditions trust your compass at all times. Easy slopes back to the old track lie in the wide arc of bearings between W and SW and you only have to avoid the steep slopes which descend into the Applecross valley at the SE. Remember that it takes about one hour to travel one mile in poor visibility. The terrain beyond Beinn a' Chla-chain is complicated and would be totally bewildering in mist.

Should you decide to use a bad morning or afternoon for compass practice (for an exercise of this sort will do you more good than sitting in your car) be warned that the Bealach na Ba road pass to Applecross (2,050ft.) can be unpleasant in thick mist, if you do not know it well. It is bad for the driver but worse for the passengers. I suggest you take the coastal road under these circumstances.

S17: An Ruadh-stac   892m   2,925ft.

O.S. sheet 25.   7-8 miles 11.3-13km.   6-7 hours.   (Map p.148 and p.156).
An Ruadh-stac (the red peak) is covered by white quartzite scree. It is the immediate southerly neighbour of the slightly higher Munro, Maoal

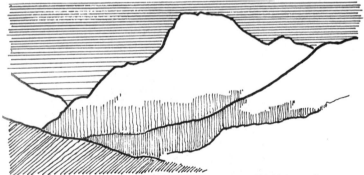

An Ruadh-stac in winter, from the Kishorn-Shieldaig road.

Chean Dearg (see map p.148). The standard route up An Ruadh-stac is via the east ridge from the bealach between these two mountains (931487) after first crossing a very rough quartzite spur south of the two small lochans at 929485. This ascent commences up easy sloping rock slabs but after 300 feet there is an abrupt increase in steepness. Above this second rock band lie steep slopes of rock and scree. The route requires a confident scrambling technique and can be dangerous when wet and in winter conditions. For the hill walker of limited experience I therefore recommend the rough but fairly easy and safe *south ridge* to the summit.

Route from the south

In the first edition of this guide I suggested a diagonal route direct towards An Ruadh-stac from the W side of the road bridge at Coulags (957451). Extended forestry planting and deer fencing (1989) have now made this approach impractical. There remain two alternative, but somewhat longer, routes from Coulags by which the south ridge can be reached. The shorter involves wading the river and the longer ascending steep but easy heather and grass slopes above the bothy at 950480. Both routes start at Coulags where you can park your car just before the bridge at (MS) 957451.

View from the summit of An Ruadh-stac looking down on the path over the bealach between An Ruadh-stac and Maol Chean Dearg (L).

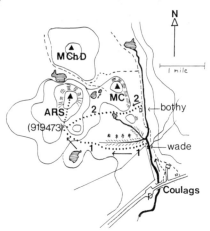

Wading route (1) Bothy route (2) to the south ridge and summit of An Ruadh-stac (ARS). Maol Chean Dearg (M Ch D) Meall nan Ceapairean (MC).

Wading Route (1)

Proceed N up the path on the E side of the river which runs down the Fionn-abhainn valley following the PUBLIC RIGHT OF WAY TO TORRIDON sign. After ¾ mile the path enters a gentle hollow (two small waterfalls ahead to your right and a few trees). You will see the deer fence extending for a further 100 yards on the other side of the river. There is a good place to wade where the main river is joined by the stream, fed by the two small waterfalls, at 953463. The flow is slower here and I have had no problems, even after rain, but you may get wet up to your knees. The stones on the river bed are slippery and a stick is helpful. Having crossed the river proceed due N for 100 yards to the end of the fence and then due W up the grassy and marshy slopes beside the deep gorge of Alt Ruigh Sleigheich on your right. At the head of this gorge, which is fed by a delightful waterfall, proceed WNW, passing S and SW of the prominent sandstone outcrop of the main mountain, then turning gradually N to reach pt. 919473.

Route from the Bothy (2)

If you prefer not to wade the river continue up the path to reach the delightfully situated bothy 1¾ miles from the road at 950480. Go through the gate in the deer fence on your left, just beyond the bothy (the upper fence is deficient and can be passed through) to ascend the tedious heather and grass slopes immediately above the bothy on your left (W). These slopes relent after 300 feet, at the horizon ridge visible above you. The slopes conquered, proceed due W across moorland, passing to the right (N) of Loch Moin a' Chriathair (937477), to avoid the more numerous lochans and streams south of this loch. Thence go WSW, up slopes, passing N of the sandstone outcrop of An Ruadh-stac to reach the same point (919473) previously described for the *wading route* (about 1½ miles and 1000 ft. from the bothy).

Looking N you are confronted by two unequal large 'bosoms' covered by quartzite scree, the right one concealing the S ridge which leads to the summit. If you make for and ascend the small mossy rake some way up the side of the left-hand 'bosom' it will keep you out of the worst of the quartzite rubble which fills the cleft between them.

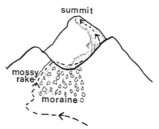

As you ascend, the great arching crest leading to the summit comes into view. Littered by quartzite rubble the ridge is wide and much easier to ascend than at first appears to be the case and numerous patches of moss-covered ground can be used to advantage. The summit cairn appears suddenly and sooner than expected. Explore the summit plateau which offers fine views, particularly of Beinn Damh to the NW (see p.118) and Maol Chean Dearg due N and the impressive view down to the bealach between Maol Chean Dearg and An Ruadh-stac with its ascending path and lochans 1000 ft below (p.155). Unless you already know this mountain well I advise you not to attempt to descend the E ridge or E face screes to gain the bealach. The rubble of quartzite on An Ruadh-stac makes one appreciate Torridonian sandstone.

S18/19: Sgurr a' Ghaoiachain and Meall Gorm
776m   2,545ft. and 710m   2,328ft.

O.S. sheet 24. Distance 2 miles 3.2km. Time 2 hours walking. (Map p.135).

The only reason for including these two peaks in ascents over 2,000ft. is because they *are* both over 2,000ft., but since your car can climb the first 2,000 feet for you, by taking you up the Bealach na Ba on the Applecross peninsula, the amount of footwork required to reach the

**Sgurr a' Ghaoiachain from Kishorn. Note the wireless mast on its
northerly peak**

summits of these eminences, which dominate the road as it ascends
the pass to left and to right, is not very great.

The summits of Sgurr a' Ghaoiachain ('Sgoorr-a-horrahhen', the
peak of the waterfall) can be reached by parking your car in the car
park placed at the highest point on the bealach (775424), walking back
down the road towards Tornapress for some 50 yards and then
ascending, on foot, up the rough vehicular track for ¾ mile to reach
the wireless mast which is situated just below the summit cairn. More
fun is to find an edge on which to park your car off the road, somewhere between the top of the zig-zags and the main car park, and free-
range up pleasant sandstone rock and grass direct to this summit.

Once there you will want to explore the top a bit and peer down into
the Corrie nan Arr. It is also worth continuing over the rough ground
beyond (east-north-east) of the wireless mast as far as you can and gaze
down the full length of precipices and gullies below you, but it is not
possible to get as far over as the Cioch itself. This is the prominent
feature one notices jutting out into the Corrie nan Arr as one ascends
the road shortly after leaving Tornapress. The great buttress of
mountain, reminiscent, in shape, of the W (Lochinver) end or
Caisteal of Suilven, which so dominates the road to the pass, and
indeed from the other side of Loch Kishorn, is cairned (797418). (See
note below.) You can extend your mountain top stroll by at least going
as far as the saddle at 790417. You must make your own decision after
that point, but that is the higher summit. (792m. 2,606ft.)

NOTE

If you just enjoy a stroll you could find this a bit 'hairy'. In fact the
ridge to the main summit is broad all the way, but an intermediate
bump requires a simple scramble in order to descend its far side. But

the ridge, although broad, has steep slopes and precipices on both sides, and the route along it, negotiating the transverse rock buttresses, is somewhat critical in places. Should inexperienced persons, without compass, become misted out (they will be at 2,500 feet) they would be caught in a potentially dangerous situation.

A large cairn at 787418 marks the beginning of the ridge to the main summit at 797418 and a good diagonal path below the rock cliff commences near a second smaller cairn 240° (direct bearing) and 55 paces SW to the right and below the main cairn. This path leads one easily to the broad ridge. Both cairns are large enough to be considered established features but they could, of course, be demolished. An intermediate hump, barring the way to the main summit, is easily ascended but requires a little, very easy, scrambling in order to descend its steep farther side. This descent is best commenced *one metre* to the right of the highest point, where a small flat ledge of rock 18 inches below the crest invites one to sit on it (although it may contain a puddle) in order then to slither safely down onto the loose rocks beneath and thence onto a steep zig-zag gravelly path and over more loose rocks to the grassy ridge beyond. Thereafter it is plain sailing to the summit cairn, but one has to descend across a broad plateau beyond the cairn in order to look down on the road to the Bealach ascending from Tornapress.

This little excursion (2 hours there and back from the Bealach) is worth doing as it affords dramatic views of the Cioch L (north) and down to Kishorn and the Bealach road R (south-east), but inexperienced shoe-clad walkers are advised not to undertake it.

Meall Gorm ('mel-gorm', *the blue hill*) dominates the SW side of the ascending road to the Bealach na Ba and its zig-zags in a series of tremendous buttresses and scree shoots. Watch out for deer in the lower part of this great valley on your left as you ascend by car from Tornapress. Leaving your vehicle at the main Bealach car park, or somewhere before then, the summit of Meall Gorm is easily and pleasantly attained over grassy and rocky ground by working your way up past the unnamed lochan near the road at 776417 and thence to the top. You may find the high wooden seat on stilts, with its roof, at about 778412, which presumably once housed some apparatus and is a fine airy place in which to repose and eat a sandwich. Beyond the summit the Meall Gorm ridge extends SE in rough but easy descending slopes for a further mile and a half, so there is plenty of ground for exploration. However, both these summits are complicated areas of rough ground and could be bewildering in mist.

The drive over the Bealach na Ba by car is easy these days since the bends were widened and barriers were erected. In winter, on a fine day, when closed to cars because of snow, the Bealach road offers a dramatic snow walk in cómparative safety and the walking distance can be satisfactorily reduced by taking the car as far as the little stone bridge at 814412; but full mountain gear should, of course, be carried under these conditions. One of the many rewards for going over the Bealach and climbing the adjacent summits are the fine views in all directions and particularly across to the Cuillin of Skye.

S20/21: Carn Breac (678m 2,224ft.) and Beinn na Feusaige (620m 2,033ft.)

O.S. sheet 25. Distance 7¹/₂ miles 12km. Time 3¹/₂-4¹/₂ hours. (Map p.161) Avoid this walk during grouse shooting (August 12- December 10).

I cannot particularly recommend this high level moorland walk, which starts and ends muddy and is somewhat featureless except for the panoramic views it offers of the mountain range to the SE (Glencarron and West Monar), N (Torridon mountains), and W (the south Torridon group). In this respect, Carn Breac (the speckled hill) offers the equivalent sweeping and grand panorama of mountains from the south that Beinn a' Chearcaill does from the north. Unpleasantly exposed and bleak in wet windy weather, these tops, including Coille Bhan and Coille Bhreac (to the east of Carn Breac) form an immense moorland horseshoe. The tops of Beinn na Feusaige and Carn Breac are good walking, but those of Coille Bhan and Coille Bhreac (the white hill and the speckled hill) which complete the horseshoe, are riven with small peat bogs and marshy ground but these do not offer any serious obstacle. You might consider this traipse for the very fine views it affords.

Leave your car just before the bridge on the Achnashellach-Achna-sheen road at 087530 (MS). Cross the bridge and find the muddy track running W up the glen on the north side of the river (Allt Coire Crubaidh). Stepping over the fence is easier than trying to open the gate. This is Forestry Commission territory and new plantations are being fenced which may cause you to modify my recommended route as time passes. The lower southern slopes of Beinn na Feusaige are, at the time of writing, churned up and fenced off. Beinn na Feusaige, a huge rounded lump with steep sides, is only just over 2,000ft. and can be omitted from the walk if preferred. If not, half a

1999: The new road has made car parking here more difficult but still practicable.

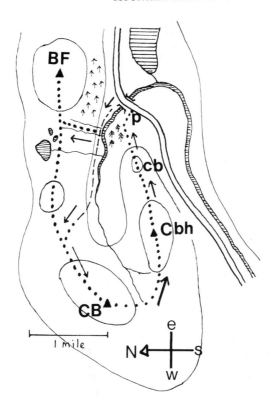

Routes for Beinn na Feusaige (BF), Carn Breac (CB), Coille Bhan (Cbh) and Coille Bhreac (cb). Park your car just south of the bridge at 087530 (p).

mile along the path there is a convenient steep grassy slope to the right between the two waterfalls which affords a stiff but easy climb to the saddle between Beinn na Feusaige and Lochan Meallan Mhic Lamhair, whence proceed E up further slopes to the summit and its lochan. Then return due W to the saddle, over Meallan Mhic Lamhair, and in a wide arc to the summit of Carn Breac.

If you prefer to omit Beinn na Feusaige (the bearded mountain) continue along the path as it ascends slowly towards the saddle W of Meallan Mhic Lamhair, free-ranging up grass slopes to the top and

161

thence to the summit of Carn Breac (045530). Numerous substantial cairns denote the activities of shooting parties but the actual summit is a survey point standing within a protective stone shrine which also protects the walker from winds as he enjoys the mountain panorama to the north-west.

The summit cairn of Carn Breac.

Carry on S from Carn Breac's summit and then, keeping to the very broad ridge, circle round S and E along the broad tops of Coille Bhan and Coille Bhreac. A host of water holes and peat bogs threaten you as you descend from Carn Breac, but they are all bluffers and are easily passed. A little path runs along the southern side of the top of the Coille Bhan and Coille Bhreac ridge, but if you find it you will lose it again as it seems to peter out. Good views of the mountains on the southern side of Glen Carron, particularly of Moruisg and Sgurr nan Ceannaichean, may be enjoyed as one strolls along this ridge. The final descent is more of a slurp than a walk, down wet grassy slopes or down the churned-up mud track created by the Forestry Commission's tractors, to a gate giving access to the road.

MAJOR RIDGE WALKS

I am only giving outline details of these major expeditions as they require experience, confidence and vigour beyond that possessed by the 'modest hill walker' and are therefore outside the intended scope of this guide. I have been on all these ridges but have only traversed parts of some of them. Experienced hill walkers can plan their own expeditions by studying the appropriate Ordnance Survey sheets (19, 24 and 25) and assess the time they will need to complete them and judge the conditions appropriate to their skills. They are full-day undertakings at heights in the 800-1050m., 2600-3400ft. range. Fuller details are given in other publications (e.g.: '*The Munros*' The Scottish Mountaineering Club Hillwalkers' Guide, ed. Bennet and '*The High Mountains*' ed. Butterfield, pub. Diadem). Some are amenable to being done in sections.

The most popular major ridges in the Torridon Region are:- Liathach; Beinn Eighe; Beinn Alligin; Beinn Liath Mhor, Sgorr Ruadh, Fuar Tholl; Beinn Dearg.

LIATHACH. East to West Traverse (O.S. Sheets 19 and 25)
Ascend via the path from the Torridon road (936566) to the saddle just W of the Stuc a' Choire Dhuibh Bhig. Thence proceed W to the main summit (Spidean a' Choire Leith) and over the dangerous pinnacles (Am Fasarinen) to the Mullach am Rathain and beyond to Sgorr a' Chadail. Thence descend due W or NW to reach the path in the Coire Mhic Nobuil leading to the Inveralligin to Torridon road (869576) six miles from the path of ascent (see pp.84-88). (No restriction during the stalking season).

BEINN EIGHE. East to West Traverse (O.S. Sheets 24 and 25)
A complete traverse of the Beinn Eighe ridges and peaks is a major undertaking. A path commences at Cromasaig on the Kinlochewe to Shieldaig road (025611) and follows the N bank of the Allt a' Chuirn towards Craig Dubh, the rough ascent of which leads to the commencement of the E to W traverse; via the Black Carls, Sgurr an Fhir Duibhe, Sgurr Ban, Spidean Coire nan Clach, A'Choianeach Mhor to Ruadh Stac Mor, the main summit. A descent to the Coire Mhic Fhearchair leads to the path via the Coire Dubh Mor to the Torridon road 5 miles W of Cromasaig. The ridge can be conveniently taken in two parts; Craig Dubh to Spidean Coire nan Clach to descend to the road via the Coire an Laoigh, and the Spidean Coire nan Clach, ascending via the Coire an Laoigh, to Ruadh Stac Mor (see pp.88-91). (No restriction during the stalking season).

BEINN ALLIGIN (O.S. Sheet 24)
Ascend via the path from the Beinn Alligin car park (869576) to gain the summit of Tom na Gruagaich. Thence follow the ridge NW to Sgurr Mhor and W to cross the Horns of Alligin, descending to gain the path in the Coire Mhic Nobuil and thence back to the car park. (see pp.91-96 for full details). This traverse is within the capabilities of the ordinary hill-walker in good weather. (No restriction during the stalking season).

BEINN LIATH MHOR, SGORR RUADH, FUAR THOLL (O.S. Sheet 25)

Take the path above Achnashellach station which ascends to the Coire Lair, leaving your car by the roadside at 005484. Take the R branch (NNE) to ascend the steep rough slopes to the eastern summit of Beinn Liath Mhor (876m., 984516). Thence follow the ridge WNW to the 925m. summit. Descend steep potentially dangerous slopes SW to the Bealach Coire Lair. Thence ascend SW to the small lochan at 954509 and SE from there to the summit of Sgorr Ruadh (960504). Descend SE to the Bhealaich Mhoir to reach the path leading back to Achnashellach, taking in the accessible summit of Fuar Tholl if desired. (see pp.140-146 for Sgorr Ruadh and Fuar Tholl and commencement of path from Achnashellach to the Coire Lair).

BEINN DEARG (O.S. Sheets 19 and 25)

Follow the path from the Beinn Alligin car park (869576) up the Coire Mhic Nobuil for 2½ miles to the Bealach a' Chomhla. Ascend the steep, potentially dangerous, terraced slopes of the western flank of the mountain to gain the summit ridge and summit. Thence E over a difficult ridge and pinnacle traverse with precipitous slopes on either side to gain the broad ridge leading ENE to Carn na Feola. Thence descend steep slopes SE to reach the path leading W back to the Coire Mhic Nobuil and the Beinn Alligin car park. Because of the difficult section immediately E of the main summit many authorities warn against attempting this traverse in bad weather (see pp.107-114).

APPENDIX

MAPS

The sketch maps are meant to help the reader identify the routes easily and not to be a substitute for taking out the proper 1:50,000 Ordnance Survey sheets (19, 24, and 25 cover the Torridon Area) when going on the mountains. I have given the mountain heights in metres and feet. The metric heights are, of course, inaccurate with respect to the last 3.28 feet. For Munros I have taken the heights, in feet, from the Munro tables. For the rest, as there is a certain amount of disagreement in various publications, I have assumed that the reader will be satisfied with a degree of approximation and I have simply multiplied the height in metres by 3.28 (which conversion factor should strictly have been 3.280843). Purists can do their own sums on this basis, but since the metre measurement itself is crude it hardly seems worth the trouble. Indispensable to world science, the metric system is a poor thing when related to human endeavour, and when I have been out all day my feet want to know how many feet they have climbed not how many metres.

GAELIC NAMES

Please take my Gaelic translations and phonetic spellings with a grain of salt. I have ravished too many publications and asked too many Highland acquaintances about word meanings to be able to give proper and due acknowledgement. On the meaning of most of the mountain names most seem to agree, but on a few there is a wide disagreement. My phonetic equivalents are a joke for, unless one is a Gael, one cannot hope to find the proper pronunciation. The *'hh'* should be taken with a soft gargle at the back of the mouth which the Scots know how to do, but the rest of us should try. Loch is *'lohh'* not lock and it is better, surely, to call the Coire Mhic Fhearchair the 'Corrie-vik-erri*hh*er', even using a Sassanach's drawl, rather than to call it, out of total ignorance, the 'Kwire-mik-fear-chair'.

EROSION

The badly eroded path up the delightful little Stac Pollaidh in Sutherland ('stac-polly', the peak of the marsh) is a warning of what happens when a mountain becomes a popular ascent, so my anxiety about popularising the, at present, sparsely visited Torridon peaks has mounted with every page that I have written. Does 'free-ranging', where there are no paths, do serious damage? Providing the walkers are few, I am sure it is actually better than wearing away existing popular routes until they become ruts, then gutters and finally great scars across the hillsides, as in Cumbria. In free-ranging one seldom, if ever, repeats oneself exactly, so that a bush of heather or a tuft of grass, if trodden on, may have five or ten years or even an eternity to recover before another chance foot lands precisely upon it. But on established paths, the boots fall remorselessly and regularly. Those arriving in Torridon to walk the mountains will do so anyway and these pages may simply divert them, with advantage, to other peaks. So I hope that this book will merely diversify but not unduly increase the pedestrian traffic upon these beautiful hills.

Respect the stalking season and enjoy good walking.

LOCAL INFORMATION

Stalking Season: Generally, late August - early November.
Grouse Shooting: August 12 - 10 December
Gairloch Conservation Unit (See maps, displayed at paths of entry)
This comprises:

> Gairloch and Conon Estate
> Grudie Estate
> National Trust for Scotland
> Forestry Commission
> Nature Conservancy Council

Outer Zone - Walking and climbing are permitted throughout the year.

Inner Zone - Please do not enter this area between **Sept 1 - 21 Nov** without obtaining permission from:

Flowerdale:	The Manager, Shieldaig Lodge Hotel.
	Tel: Badachro 741250
Slatterdale:	Forester. Tel: Achnashellach 766273
Glen Grudie:	Grudie House (Mr. J. Wills).
	Tel Kinlochewe 760259
Nature Reserve:	Warden Tel: Kinlochewe 760359

South West Ross Deer Management Group
(Deer Stalking: Mid August - Mid October)
Estate Contact Numbers:

Applecross	01520 744247/733249
Kinloch	01520 755206
Ben Shieldaig	01445 791343/ 01520 733227
Couldoran	01520 733227
Ben Damph	01445 791252/791289
Coulin	01445 760383
Tullich	01520 733227
New Kelso	01349 864419
Fionnaraich	01520 766236
Achnashellach	01520 766266
Glencarron	01520 766275
Ledgowan	01445 720209

A map showing the location of these estates is displayed at Annat (at the commencement of the signposted path to Coulags). O.S. Sheet 24. 894544.

MOUNTAIN RESCUE: Torridon S.Y.H.A. Tel: 01445 791284

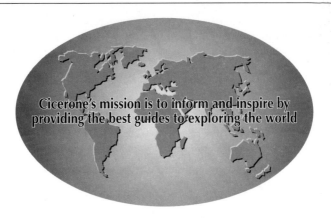

Cicerone's mission is to inform and inspire by providing the best guides to exploring the world

Since its foundation over 30 years ago, Cicerone has specialised in publishing guidebooks and has built a reputation for quality and reliability. It now publishes nearly 300 guides to the major destinations for outdoor enthusiasts, including Europe, UK and the rest of the world.

Written by leading and committed specialists, Cicerone guides are recognised as the most authoritative. They are full of information, maps and illustrations so that the user can plan and complete a successful and safe trip or expedition – be it a long face climb, a walk over Lakeland fells, an alpine traverse, a Himalayan trek or a ramble in the countryside.

With a thorough introduction to assist planning, clear diagrams, maps and colour photographs to illustrate the terrain and route, and accurate and detailed text, Cicerone guides are designed for ease of use and access to the information.

If the facts on the ground change, or there is any aspect of a guide that you think we can improve, we are always delighted to hear from you.

Cicerone Press
2 Police Square Milnthorpe Cumbria LA7 7PY
Tel:01539 562 069   Fax:01539 563 417
e-mail:info@cicerone.co.uk   web:www.cicerone.co.uk